WEB DESIGN: E-COMMERCE

Ed. Julius Wiedemann

TASCHEN

HONG KONG KÖLN LONDON LOS ANGELES MADRID PARIS TOKYO

CONTENTS

90052

Library & Learning Centre
University for the Creative Arts
Farnham

Introduction
Julius Wiedemann

Have you ever bought online? Or better, how often do you buy online? Even if you have never bought online, you know that in fact all the stuff available to us "offline" is managed and mostly ordered online. Some years ago, with the rise of broadband and the popularisation of digital means of communication such as e-mail and instant messaging, many people and internet experts advocated the "death" of postal services. But what has actually happened is that these services, alongside credit card operators, became the big enablers of global e-commerce. Millions of small packages are sent out everyday to customers in all corners of the globe, containing all kinds of goods.

It doesn't matter today if you are big or small, if you sell your own t-shirts or have an astrology portal. You can both start a purely online business or you can adapt your business to an online distribution model. The doors are open to everyone. Internet democratised not only the information flow but also the distribution channels. Selling online has some 'special effects' so to speak. First of all you are able to sell globally, which is great. If you are in Germany, it is only a matter of time that stands between you receiving an order from Malaysia, Japan, India, etc. The rules are the same regardless of whether you are in Japan, United States or Argentina. The borders are gone. And on the other hand, if you start something online, you should be prepared to satisfy consumers' needs quickly. On the web, that basically means being fast. You also need to have your logistics prepared beforehand. And provide information to avoid having to answer any doubts, etc. Doing your homework, or having your company do it is fundamental. This book

was also designed to help you on this side. The tone is: be prepared, not afraid!

There are examples where being online is the only way. Take the case of software. The whole process is digital. It is produced digitally, can be marketed digitally and distributed the same way. This perspective enables thousands of independent programmers and small software companies to develop their ideas and solutions for specific problems and to deliver directly to customers. At TASCHEN, we had a partnership with online shops to sell our books online for a long time, but we changed that a couple years ago by selling them ourselves, and moreover, our content website became totally integrated with the online shop. These days, nobody talks about online as "virtual" anymore. Years ago we had virtual this, virtual that, and online commerce was in this category as well. But now it is as real as ever. This book brings you more than 50 different examples of online shops that have achieved a very high degree of incorporation of design, the focus of this series, with good interface and practical methods for shopping. Moreover, we have added sites with innovation in the previously mentioned topics.

You will not find here some of the most commented on and used e-commerce sites such as amazon.com or dell. com, people that also innovated and today make big business online. And the reason for them not to be there is simple. We wanted to fill the pages of the book with examples of sites that you might never have heard of, and we hope that their approach to online commerce helps you somehow. Maybe there is a good idea for you to start a business, there might be an insight to improve what you already have or simply a good bench-marketing for you.

Every project comes with a set of information that has marked this series. Information that you usually do not find everywhere, such as the design office respon-sible for the design, the numbers of hours, the awards won by the site, etc. We have also decided to feature a bigger number of more detailed case studies, in order to give to every reader the opportunity to know more about seven different stories of successful e-commerce projects, with in depth information. The stories come from diverse business, to exemplify that from bicycles to prints to photography, everyone can do good business online. Carry also this book with you to remember your friends and colleagues about many of the nice things you have found here. Have a nice trip!

Introduction
Julius Wiedemann

Avez-vous déjà fait des achats en ligne ? Même si vous ne l'avez jamais fait, vous savez que tout ce que l'on trouve dans le commerce est le plus souvent géré et commandé par Internet. Il y a quelques années, avec l'essor du haut débit et la popularisation des moyens de communication numérique comme l'e-mail et la messagerie instantanée, de nombreux experts et non-experts ont prédit la « mort » des services postaux. Mais ce qui est arrivé, c'est que les services postaux, ainsi que les opérateurs de cartes de crédit, sont devenus des instruments essentiels pour l'e-commerce global. Chaque jour, dans le monde entier, des millions de clients reçoivent des millions de petits colis qui renferment toutes sortes de produits.

Que votre entreprise soit grande ou petite, que vous vendiez vos propres T-shirts ou que vous ayez un site d'astrologie, peu importe. Vous pouvez soit monter une entreprise entièrement sur Internet, soit adapter votre entreprise à un modèle de distribution en ligne. Les portes sont ouvertes à tout le monde. Internet a démocratisé non seulement le flux d'informations, mais aussi les canaux de distribution.

Vendre sur Internet a certains effets spéciaux, si l'on peut dire. Tout d'abord, cela vous permet de vendre dans le monde entier, ce qui n'est pas rien. Si vous êtes en Allemagne, vous finirez toujours par recevoir une commande de la Malaisie, du Japon, de l'Inde, etc. Si vous êtes au Japon, les États-Unis ou l'Argentine seront aussi vos clients. Il n'y a plus de frontières. Et de l'autre côté, si vous montez quelque chose sur Internet, il faudra être prêt à satisfaire les besoins du consommateur rapidement. Il faudra aussi que votre logistique soit bien huilée. Et puis il faudra fournir assez d'informations pour éviter de devoir répondre à de nombreuses questions, etc. La préparation est fondamentale. Ce livre a aussi été conçu pour vous aider de ce côté-là. Le mot d'ordre est : soyez préparé, pas effrayé !

Il y a des cas où Internet est la seule solution. Prenez l'exemple des logiciels. Tout le processus est numérique. La production d'un logiciel est numérique, son marketing et sa distribution peuvent l'être aussi. Cela permet à des milliers de programmateurs indépendants et de petites entreprises de développer leurs idées et leurs solutions à des problèmes spécifiques et de les livrer directement aux clients. Chez TASCHEN, nous avions depuis longtemps mis en place un partenariat avec des boutiques en ligne pour vendre nos livres sur Internet. Mais nous l'avons modifié il y a quelques années afin de pouvoir vendre nos livres nous-mêmes, et pour intégrer notre propre site à la boutique en ligne.

De nos jours, plus personne ne qualifie la sphère Internet de « virtuelle ». Il y a quelques années, c'était virtuel par-ci, virtuel par-là, et le commerce sur Internet tombait aussi dans cette catégorie. Mais maintenant tout cela est plus réel que jamais. Ce livre présente plus de cinquante exemples de boutiques en ligne qui ont non seulement un excellent design, le thème central de cette série, mais aussi une bonne interface et des méthodes d'achat pratiques. De plus, nous avons ajouté des sites qui innovent dans les sujets mentionnés ci-dessus.

Certains des sites d'e-commerce les plus connus et les plus utilisés, comme amazon.com ou dell.com, qui ont également innové et font aujourd'hui de gros chiffres d'affaires sur Internet, sont absents de cet ouvrage. Et la raison en est bien simple. Nous voulions remplir les pages de ce livre avec des exemples de sites dont vous pourriez n'avoir jamais entendu parler, et nous espérons que leur manière d'aborder le commerce en ligne vous inspire. Ce peut être une bonne idée pour monter une entreprise, pour améliorer ce que vous avez déjà, ou simplement un bon point de comparaison pour vous.

Chaque projet est accompagné d'un ensemble d'informations pour lesquelles cette série est célèbre. Des informations que l'on ne trouve pas partout, comme le bureau de design responsable du projet, le nombre d'heures, les récompenses que le site a reçues, etc. Nous avons aussi décidé de présenter un plus grand nombre d'études de cas afin de vous permettre de connaître en profondeur l'histoire de sept projets d'e-commerce couronnés de succès. Ces études de cas illustrent divers secteurs pour montrer que, des velos à la photographie, en passant par l'impression, tout le monde peut faire des affaires sur Internet.

Emportez ce livre avec vous pour montrer à vos amis et à vos collègues les projets intéressants que vous aurez trouvés ici. Bon voyage !

Einleitung
Julius Wiedemann

Haben Sie schon einmal im Internet eingekauft? Und wie oft nutzen Sie das Internet für Einkäufe? Auch wenn Sie noch nie etwas online gekauft haben, wissen Sie sicherlich, dass alles, was offline erhältlich ist, zu einem großen Teil online verwaltet und bestellt wird. Als vor einigen Jahren Breitbandverbindungen aufkamen und digitale Kommunikationsmittel wie E-Mail und Instant Messaging sich ausbreiteten, sagten viele das Ende der Postdienste voraus. Tatsächlich jedoch machten diese, gemeinsam mit den Kreditkartenanbietern, den globalen E-Commerce erst möglich. Millionen von Päckchen mit allen erdenklichen Produkten werden jeden Tag zu Kunden auf der ganzen Welt geliefert.

Heute ist es nicht wichtig, wie groß ein Unternehmen ist, ob man selbst angefertigte T-Shirts verkauft oder ein Internetportal für Astrologie betreibt. Man kann ein reines Internetgeschäft führen oder sein Unternehmen auf den Online-Vertrieb umstellen. Jeder hat die gleichen Möglichkeiten. Das Internet hat nicht nur den Informationsfluss demokratisiert, sondern auch die Vertriebswege.

Der Verkauf über das Internet ist von einigen Besonderheiten gekennzeichnet: Zunächst einmal kann man weltweit verkaufen. Hat man seinen Sitz in Deutschland, so ist es nur eine Frage der Zeit, bis man Bestellungen aus Malaysia, Japan oder Indien erhält. Das gleiche gilt für Unternehmen in Japan, den USA oder Argentinien. Es gibt keine Grenzen mehr. Das heißt auch, dass man darauf vorbereitet sein sollte, die Wünsche der Kunden schnell zu erfüllen. Auch die Logistik muss gut funktionieren. Stellen Sie Informationen zur Verfügung, um häufige Anfragen zu vermeiden. Dies sind wesentliche Voraussetzungen für den Erfolg. Das vorliegende Buch möchte Ihnen dabei behilflich sein. Seien Sie nicht ängstlich, sondern gut vorbereitet!

In manchen Fällen gibt es keine Alternative zum Internet. Dies betrifft zum Beispiel Software, bei der alle Abläufe digital sind: Sie wird digital hergestellt, kann digital vermarktet und vertrieben werden. Unabhängige Programmierer und kleine Software-Unternehmen können Ideen und Lösungsvorschläge entwickeln und diese den Kunden direkt zur Verfügung stellen. Bei TASCHEN hatten wir lange eine Kooperation mit Online-Shops, um unsere Bücher über das Internet zu vertreiben. Seit einigen Jahren verkaufen wir sie jedoch selbst und haben den Online-Shop in unsere Internetseite integriert.

Heute spricht beim Thema Internet niemand mehr von „virtuell". Früher war dies ein viel benutzter Begriff, der auch auf das Online-Geschäft angewandt wurde. Dabei ist dieses sehr real. Dieses Buch stellt mehr als 50 verschiedene Online-Shops vor, denen eine ausgezeichnete Verbindung von Design, das im Mittelpunkt dieser Reihe steht, einer benutzerfreundlichen Oberfläche und zweckmäßigen Einkaufs-Tools gelungen ist. Zusätzlich werden Websites vorgestellt, die sich durch besondere Innovationen in den erwähnten Bereichen auszeichnen.

Was Sie hier nicht finden werden, sind erfolgreiche und ebenfalls innovative E-Commerce-Seiten wie amazon.com und dell.com. Der Grund dafür ist einfach: Wir wollten in diesem Buch Websites vorstellen, die Sie möglicherweise noch nicht kennen, und wir hoffen, dass deren Beispiel Ihnen hilfreich sein wird. Sei es, dass es Sie auf eine gute Unternehmensidee bringt, Ihnen Einsichten verschafft, wie Sie Ihr Unternehmen

verbessern können, oder Ihnen einfach die Möglichkeit
zum Vergleich gibt.

Wie immer in dieser Reihe sind jedem Projekt
Informationen beigefügt, die Sie nicht überall finden, wie
etwa zum Designbüro, zur Anzahl der Arbeitsstunden
oder zu den Auszeichnungen, die die Seite erhalten hat.
Wir haben uns außerdem dazu entschlossen, detaillierte
Fallstudien mit ausführlichen Hintergrundinformationen
einzufügen, um Ihnen die Möglichkeit zu geben, mehr
über die Erfolgsgeschichten von sieben E-Commerce-
Projekten zu erfahren. Die Geschichten stammen aus
unterschiedlichen Branchen, um zu veranschaulichen,
dass das Online-Geschäft allen offen steht, ob es nun um
Fahrräder, Printmedien oder Fotos geht.

Zeigen Sie Ihren Freunden und Kollegen, was Sie in
diesem Buch alles entdeckt haben. Wir wünschen Ihnen
viel Erfolg!

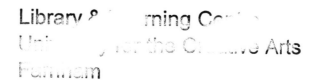

O'Neill Website
2Advanced Studios

THE CHALLENGE. Back in the 1950s, Jack O'Neill set up his first surf shop and invented the modern-day surfing wetsuit, becoming one of the leading pioneers in the early Californian surf scene. Therefore, when O'Neill, Inc. approached 2Advanced Studios to redesign and develop its website, the 2Advanced team knew it had to raise the bar in terms of design, functionality, and backend development. The new O'Neill website needed to appeal to a highly discerning target audience, while also paying homage to one of surfing's best known and respected brands.

THE SOLUTION. The 2Advanced team created an edgy, innovative design that highlights the fun-loving spirit of the O'Neill brand as well as the carefree vibe of the action sports industry. To accomplish this, the 2Advanced team departed from the traditional, technological tone of most e-commerce websites. Instead, the team opted for a more organic, beach-themed color palette consisting of oceanic blues and sandy beiges. The end result is an aesthetic that truly captures O'Neill's Southern California style.

To showcase O'Neill's diverse array of products and gear, 2Advanced Studios developed dedicated sections for both genders and each of the various sports genres. Each subsection boasts entirely distinctive designs to keep users stimulated with fresh stimuli, encouraging them to fully explore the breadth of content, and thus reinforcing O'Neill's content strategy.

The innovative navigational metaphor is easy to follow, promotes visitors to interact with the site's numerous features, and minimizes while not is use. The highly functional metaphor lets visitors choose from "Men" or "Juniors/Women," and then further narrows down the product search by specific sport (Surf, Wake, Snow, and Other).

However, 2Advanced Studios fully understand that a great website incorporates more than just great design. Therefore, the development team also built a new relational database for O'Neill along with a customized content management system which drives almost every page of the website. Now O'Neill can quickly and efficiently upload new content, video and other rich media.

The project was further enhanced with the launch of the interactive custom wetsuit and boardshort builders. These Flash-based modules enable visitors to fully customize and purchase their own wetsuit and boardshort by selecting from numerous options for style, color schemes, graphics, patterns and sizes.

The 2Advanced development team utilized object oriented programming to create the intuitive, easy-to-use process, which utilizes a product viewer to show customers' progress as they "try-on" the various options. With tons of unique combinations, customers can take their time to create their ultimate wetsuit or boardshort. Once the check out process is complete, the customized order is then sent to a database for easy online viewing by the manufacturer and customer.

Considering the accelerated timeframe for the project, the 2Advanced development team worked overtime to ensure the modules utilized clean code, provided an accurate representation of the end product, and were easy to use. Since the launch, no bugs or issues have been encountered proving that the extra development time and attention to detail were well spent.

www.oneill.com

This was the first time O'Neill customers were given the opportunity to customize their own O'Neill products prior to purchase. Considering O'Neill's premiere positioning within the industry, the builders' instant popularity was of little surprise.

THE IMPACT. Bret Muhlitner, Director of Marketing for O'Neill, Inc., said, "We wanted a website that offered an engaging experience and centralized product content worldwide. 2Advanced Studios not only delivered on these goals, they substantially bolstered our online market presence. The added interactive features and innovative design went beyond our overall expectations."

The O'Neill website received a Gold Award in the Marcom Creative Awards, an Outstanding Award in HOW Magazine's Interactive Design Awards, and "Site of the Day" recognitions from Macromedia.com and Favourite Website Awards (FWA).

About **2Advanced Studios**, LLC. Founded in 1999, by Co-Founders, Eric Jordan and Tony Novak, 2Advanced Studios has quickly evolved into an award-winning interactive agency with nearly 30 employees in the United States and Japan. World renowned for their creative talents in Macromedia Flash design, 2Advanced also offers a wide range of design and development services, including interactive design, development and backend solutions, broadcast video, 3D graphics, multimedia, identity and audio production. 2Advanced is highly noted for its contributions to several major book publications, as well as a wide array of magazine articles, online interviews and industry awards. Located in Aliso Viejo, California, the 2Advanced team constantly strives to push the creative boundaries of technology to deliver high impact new media solutions that create a lasting impression. For more information, visit <**www.2advanced.com**>.

O'Neill Website
2 Advanced Studios

LE DÉFI. C'est dans les années 1950 que Jack O'Neill a créé son premier magasin de surf, a inventé la combinaison de surf moderne, et est devenu l'un des plus grands pionniers de la sphère du surf en Californie. C'est pourquoi, lorsque O'Neill, Inc. a demandé à 2 Advanced Studios de revoir le design de son site et de le développer, l'équipe de 2 Advanced savait qu'il faudrait placer la barre plus haut en termes de design, de fonctionnalité et de développement d'interface administrateur. Le nouveau site O'Neill devait plaire à un public très exigeant et rendre hommage à l'une des marques les plus connues et les plus respectées du monde du surf.

LA SOLUTION. L'équipe de 2 Advanced a créé un site dynamique et innovant qui met en valeur l'esprit ludique de la marque O'Neill et l'atmosphère détendue du secteur des sports d'action. Pour cela, l'équipe de 2 Advanced s'est éloignée du ton traditionnel et technologique de la plupart des sites d'e-commerce. L'équipe a préféré une palette de couleurs plus organique, sur le thème de la plage, composée de bleus océan et de beiges sable. Le résultat est une esthétique qui saisit vraiment style californien d'O'Neill.

Pour présenter le large éventail de produits et d'équipements d'O'Neill, les studios 2 Advanced ont créé des sections différentes pour chaque sexe et chaque type de sport. Comme chaque sous-section est complètement différente des autres, les utilisateurs reçoivent constamment de nouveaux stimuli et sont encouragés à explorer tout le site, ce qui renforce la stratégie de contenu d'O'Neill.

La métaphore de navigation est innovante et facile à suivre. Elle encourage les visiteurs à interagir avec les nombreuses fonctions du site et se met en retrait lorsqu'elle n'est pas utilisée. Cette métaphore très fonctionnelle permet aux visiteurs de choisir entre « Hommes » ou « Juniors/Femmes », puis d'affiner la recherche de produits par sport (surf, wake, snow, et autres).

Mais les studios 2 Advanced savaient aussi que, pour faire un bon site, il fallait davantage qu'un bon concept. L'équipe de développement a donc construit pour O'Neill une nouvelle base de données relationnelle ainsi qu'un système personnalisé de gestion des contenus qui administre presque toutes les pages du site. Maintenant, O'Neill peut télécharger rapidement et efficacement de nouveaux contenus multimédias sur son site.

Le projet a encore été amélioré avec le lancement d'applications interactives de création de combinaisons et de shorts personnalisés. Ces modules en Flash permettent aux visiteurs d'acheter une combinaison ou un short complètement personnalisé : ils peuvent choisir parmi une généreuse sélection de styles, de couleurs, de graphismes, de motifs et de tailles.

L'équipe de développement de 2 Advanced a utilisé la programmation par objets pour créer ce processus intuitif et facile à utiliser, qui permet aux clients de voir l'état d'avancement du produit pendant qu'ils essaient les différentes options. Le grand nombre de combinaisons possibles permet aux clients de prendre leur temps pour créer la combinaison ou le short qui leur ira comme un gant. Au terme de ce processus, la commande personnalisée est envoyée vers une base de données que le fabricant et le client peuvent consulter facilement en ligne.

L'équipe de développement de 2 Advanced a fait des

heures supplémentaires pour respecter les échéances serrées du projet et s'assurer que les modules fonctionnent avec un code impeccable, donnent une représentation fidèle du produit final, et soient faciles à utiliser. Aucun bug ni aucun problème n'ont été rencontrés depuis le lancement, ce qui prouve que le temps supplémentaire de développement et de vérification des détails n'a pas été en vain.

C'était la première fois que les clients d'O'Neill avaient l'occasion de personnaliser leurs produits avant de les acheter. Étant donné la position d'O'Neill comme leader dans le secteur, la popularité instantanée des modules n'a pas été une grande surprise.

L'IMPACT. Bret Muhliner, directeur de marketing chez O'Neill, Inc., a déclaré « Nous voulions un site captivant et interactif avec un contenu produit centralisé pour le monde entier. Les studios 2Advanced n'ont pas seulement respecté ces objectifs, ils ont considérablement renforcé notre présence sur Internet. L'interactivité des fonctions supplémentaires et l'originalité du design ont dépassé nos attentes. »

Le site O'Neill a reçu un Gold Award des prix Marcom Creative, un Outstanding Award des prix Interactive Design du magazine HOW, et a été élu « site du jour » par Macromedia.com et Favourite Website Awards (FWA).

À propos des studios **2Advanced**, LLC. Fondés en 1999 par les co-fondateurs Eric Jordan et Tony Novak, les studios 2Advanced sont rapidement devenus une agence interactive primée, avec près de 30 employés aux États-Unis et au Japon. Reconnus dans le monde entier pour leur créativité dans l'utilisation de Macromedia Flash, les studios 2Advanced proposent également un large éventail de services de design et de développement : design interactif, solutions d'interface administrateur et développement, diffusion de vidéo, graphismes en 3D, multimédia, identité et production audio. 2Advanced a contribué à plusieurs livres importants, ainsi qu'à de nombreux articles de magazines, entretiens en ligne et récompenses dans leur domaine d'activité. Située à Aliso Viejo, en Californie, l'équipe de 2Advanced cherche sans cesse à repousser les limites créatives de la technologie pour fournir de nouvelles solutions média qui laissent une empreinte durable. Pour de plus amples informations, visitez <www.2advanced.com>.

O'Neill Website
2 Advanced Studios

DIE AUFGABE. In den 1950er Jahren eröffnete Jack O'Neill seinen ersten Surfshop, erfand den modernen Surfanzug und wurde zu einem der führenden Pioniere der frühen kalifornischen Surfszene. Als 2 Advanced damit beauftragt wurde, die Website der Firma O'Neill neu zu gestalten, war klar, dass man neue Standards in Sachen Design, Funktionalität und Backend-Entwicklung setzen musste. Die neue Seite musste eine anspruchsvolle Zielgruppe ansprechen und gleichzeitig einer der bekanntesten Surfermarken Tribut zollen.

DIE LÖSUNG. Das Team von 2 Advanced entwarf ein prägnantes, innovatives Design, das sowohl den „funloving spirit" der Marke O'Neill reflektiert als auch die positive Ausstrahlung der Actionsport-Industrie. So ließ man die technische Anmutung der meisten E-Commerce-Seiten hinter sich und entschied sich statt dessen für eine lebendige Farbpalette aus Meeresblau und Sandfarben. Daraus entstand eine Ästhetik, die den „Southern California Style" von O'Neill exakt widerspiegelt.

Für die Präsentation des vielfältigen Produktangebots von O'Neill entwickelte 2 Advanced spezifische Bereiche für Männer und Frauen sowie für die verschiedenen Sportarten. Jedes Untermenü verfügt über ein eigenes Design, um die User mit immer neuen Eindrücken zu unterhalten und sie anzuregen, die gesamte Website zu entdecken. Auf diese Weise wird die Content-Strategie von O'Neill untermauert.

Das bildhafte Navigationsmenü ist leicht verständlich, lädt dazu ein, die zahlreichen Features auszuprobieren und wird bei Nichtgebrauch minimiert dargestellt. Die Kunden können zwischen den Kategorien „Men" und „Juniors/Women" wählen, und die Produktsuche dann auf bestimmte Sportarten eingrenzen (Surf, Wake, Snow und Other).

Die Mitarbeiter von 2 Advanced waren sich aber auch darüber im Klaren, dass eine herausragende Website mehr braucht als ein herausragendes Design. So baute das Entwicklerteam auch eine neue Relationale Datenbank für O'Neill auf, zusammen mit einem spezifischen Content-Management-System, das fast jeder Seite zugrunde liegt. Somit kann O'Neill nun schnell und effizient neuen Content, Videos und andere Rich-Media-Anwendungen hochladen.

Eine weitere Verbesserung stellte die Einführung der interaktiven Elemente „wetsuit builder" und „boardshort builder" dar. Diese auf Flash basierenden Module geben den Kunden die Möglichkeit, sich ihre Surfanzüge und -shorts selbst zusammenzustellen, indem sie Style, Farben, Grafik, Muster und Größen aus zahlreichen Möglichkeiten auswählen.

Das Team von 2 Advanced nutzte objektorientiertes Programmieren, um den leicht verständlichen Auswahlvorgang zu gestalten, bei dem eine Produktvorschau den Fortschritt der Kunden anzeigt, während diese verschiedene Varianten „anprobieren". Die Kunden können aus einer Vielzahl von Kombinationsmöglichkeiten die für sie perfekten Surfanzüge oder Shorts zusammenstellen. Dann wird die Bestellung an eine Datenbank übermittelt, so dass Hersteller und Kunde den aktuellen Stand online ansehen können.

Das Entwicklerteam von 2 Advanced machte viele Überstunden, um sicherzustellen, dass die Module reinen Code benutzten, das Endprodukt exakt darstellten und einfach zu benutzen waren. Seit dem Launch der Website

sind keine Bugs oder anderen Probleme aufgetreten, womit der Beweis erbracht ist, dass die zusätzliche Entwicklungszeit und die Konzentration auf Details sich gelohnt haben.

Dies war das erste Mal, dass Kunden von O'Neill die Möglichkeit erhielten, die Produkte vor dem Kauf individuell zu gestalten. Bedenkt man die herausragende Stellung von O'Neill in der Sportartikel-Branche, so überrascht es nicht, dass der interaktive „Builder" sofort ein gr ußer Erfolg war.

DIE WIRKUNG. Bret Muhlitner, Marketingleiter von O'Neill, sagte: „Wir wollten eine spannende Website, die ein weltweit zentralisiertes Produktangebot bieten würde. 2Advanced haben diese Zielsetzung nicht nur erfüllt, sie haben unsere Online-Präsenz auch wesentlich gestärkt. Die zusätzlichen interaktiven Features und das innovative Design haben all unsere Erwartungen übertroffen."

Die Website von O'Neill wurde mit dem Gold Award der Marcom Creative Awards und dem Outstanding Award der Interactive Design Awards der Zeitschrift HOW ausgezeichnet. Außerdem wurde sie von Macromedia. com und Favourite Website Awards (FWA) zur „Site of the Day" gewählt.

2Advanced Studios, 1999 von Eric Jordan und Tony Novak gegründet, hat sich schnell zu einer preisgekrönten Multimedia-Agentur mit fast 30 Mitarbeitern in den USA und Japan entwickelt. Die Agentur ist nicht nur weltweit anerkannt für ihre kreativen Leistungen in Macromedia Flash Design, sondern bietet auch ein großes Spektrum von Dienstleistungen im Bereich Design und Entwicklung an. 2Advanced veröffentlichte mit großem Erfolg Bücher und Zeitschriftenartikel, gab Online-Interviews und wurde mit Branchenpreisen ausgezeichnet. Die Mitarbeiter von 2Advanced setzen sich beständig dafür ein, die Grenzen zu verschieben, die der Kreativität durch die Technik gesetzt werden. Ihr Ziel sind wirksame Multimedia-Lösungen, die einen bleibenden Eindruck hinterlassen. Mehr Informationen unter <www.2advanced.com>.

Victoria's Secret Website
Firstborn

SEXY SELLS. When clients like Victoria's Secret come knocking on your door you can't afford an out-of-the-box design solution – it has to be fresh and unconventional. Thankfully, their advertising campaigns always provide ideal inspiration – beautiful photos of beautiful women in beautiful clothing! With Victoria's Secret, there are no limits on sexy.

Every time Firstborn approaches a new interface design we think of a graphic device that can turn into an interactive hook. To date, we have worked on three major launches; Victoria's Secret: Blue London Jean in 2003, IPEX™ in 2005, and the 10th Anniversary of the Swim Collection in 2005. All three projects consisted of designing a mini-site that lived within the existing Victoria's Secret website. Each had to be its own experience that intimately translated the brand message in an exciting new way – and naturally, the mini-site gave us ample room to be creative and experiment with unconventional design and navigation.

DIGITAL DENIM. To re-launch its denim collection, Blue London Jean, Victoria's Secret charged Firstborn with creating a sophisticated site that would extend the sensuality of the brand while conveying practical information about the jeans.

In this case, the first thing we noticed about the client's images (besides being irresistibly sexy) was that they could easily be turned into silhouettes. The model silhouettes resembled letterforms when they lined up. Letters and words are the world's most common navigation devices and this train of thought led us to consider using the images themselves as a primary means of navigating the site.

Another design device was the vertical line that followed the mouse and defined the edge of the mask that concealed part of the image. This solution kept all models in plain view and made the bigger image more intriguing. Likewise, this led to a visually exciting "reveal" effect that, with the simple move of the mouse, allowed users to see detailed views of the eight styles of jeans and the twelve different washes.

After the interactive hook for the "Style Index" became reasonably clear we started thinking of putting a different twist on it for the "Style Detail" page. We decided to turn the layout 90 degrees and make the "reveal" line horizontal. This allowed for the mask to reveal an enlarged view of a model.

We projected the same logic on the other half of the experience – "Wash Index" and "Wash Detail" pages. By adding cross-links throughout the site, virtually any piece of content becomes available from any given point. To complete the 4-way symmetry of the site we placed the "Blue London Jean" logo in 4 different quadrants to emphasize structural equilibrium.

Feminine lines, sensual curves, perfect fit for lots of shapes and sizes; twelve different washes, eight great styles and one sexy denim collection presented in a digital medium.

Innovative and informative, sexy and simple to use, the Blue London Jean website provided an auspicious digital debut of the denim collection for Victoria's Secret.

THE SEXY REVOLUTION. Who says that technology cannot be sexy, sensual, or for that matter a huge hit for a new bra? 2005 started off with the introduction of a revolutionary bra called IPEX™. For those of you who are

BLUE LONDON JEAN

THE
BOYFRIEND
The Boyfriend buttonfly. The comfort of this jean was designed for you.
▶ SEE DETAILS

Available in these washes:

▶ SEE ALL 12 WASHES

curious, it's a super lightweight bra that uses the latest in digital and laser technology.

To support the launch of the world's most advanced bra, Firstborn had to create an all Flash interactive experience that told the story of IPEX™ – of course we had a little help from supermodel Gisele Bundchen. Once again, the interface was inspired by the photographs of the model taken on a black background, but we took it beyond the photos, and we imagined a universe made up of Gisele constellations... and no matter which part of the universe you wanted to visit, you had to travel through nebulous space to get there. Translated into Flash, this experience felt like an ultra-zoom that had you flying by images of Gisele in a dark space.

The IPEX™ project consisted of two phases: the March launch and the August re-launch, which was much smaller in scale. The second design for IPEX™ took its inspiration from the energy-filled commercials that Victoria's Secret produced featuring models dancing on a stage in front of a huge IPEX™ logo. The intro sequence used a mesh-like texture to illustrate high-tech sexy, and the transitions depicted a spotlight circling the stage. We were going for a theatrical experience that projected enough energy and sexy into the brand message.

A major success for Victoria's Secret, the launch of the IPEX™ bra was accompanied by large billboards, tv spots, and magazine spreads. This interactive campaign educated the consumer and emphasized the importance of technology for the brand.

10 YEARS OF SEXY. 2005 marked the 10th an-

niversary of Victoria's Secret's Swim Collection. To com-
memorate a decade of success, style and sexy, Victoria's
Secret hosted an event and published an exclusive book,
SEXY, featuring the works of three photographers who
captured the collection's essence. Following the event,
Firstborn developed a commemorative mini-site which
featured exclusive footage from behind the scenes of
the swim shoot, photographs from the party as well as
editorial content for the press and public.

Initially, we thought about creating a sexy "fun in the
sun" type of experience for this piece, but ultimately a
sexier, sultrier, and more alluring experience was called
for. The photographs supplied for the project were
beyond our wildest imagination – and so we focused on
creating a memorable photo gallery. Sure, the photos
themselves were memorable enough, but we wanted
to make "flipping" through them also noteworthy. In
this piece users can preview any photo by rolling over
the corresponding number and see a thumbnail appear
either in the top right corner or to the lower left corner
of the current photo, depending on where in the number
line she is looking. It seems so simple when explained,
but the effect was an unusual toggle-like navigation that
was easily adapted to the video gallery, and made the
experience more than just a linear click-through.

The online campaign did a great job of supporting the
event, and letting people know that Victoria's Secret
Swim Collection was hotter than ever. VIPs were presented with a special book commemorating the decade of
beautiful swimwear and the models that sported them.

We can honestly say that working on these Victoria's
Secret projects has been very rewarding creatively. Our

design aesthetic merged seamlessly with the gorgeous
assets provided to us by the client, resulting in online
campaigns with equal parts sex appeal and functionality.

Firstborn is a New York based interactive agency founded in
1997. Firstborn has been producing award winning interactive
and print design over the years for high-profile clients in various
industries. <www.firstbornmultimedia.com>

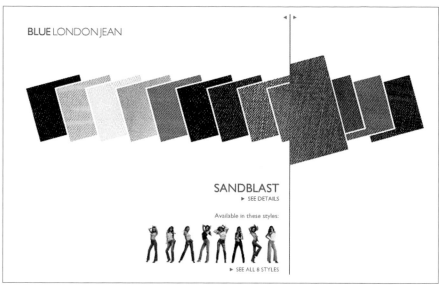

BLUE LONDON JEAN

SANDBLAST
▶ SEE DETAILS

Available in these styles:

▶ SEE ALL 8 STYLES

THE
FRAY
Frayed edges.
No waist.
No back pockets.
Shown in Sandblast.

Available in these washes:

▶ SEE ALL 12 WASHES
▶ SEE ALTERNATE VIEW

▶ BUY NOW

BLUE LONDON JEAN

THE
FRAY
Frayed edges.
No waist.
No back pockets.
Shown in Sandblast.

RISE
Very low. 7" - 9" between
the top of the waistband and
the crotch seam.

HIP
Fitted through the hip
and thigh.

LEG
Flare leg with
gusset details.

▶ BUY NOW

BLUE LONDON JEAN

VINTAGE WASH
Shown: The Fray

Available in these styles

▶ SEE ALL 8 STYLES

BLUE LONDON JEAN

VINTAGE WASH
Shown: The Fray

Available in these styles

▶ SEE ALL 8 STYLES

BLUE LONDON JEAN

Victoria's Secret Website
Firstborn

LA SÉDUCTION FAIT VENDRE. Lorsqu'un client comme Victoria's Secret frappe à votre porte, il n'est pas question de piocher dans le tiroir aux idées, il faut proposer de l'inédit et du non conventionnel. Heureusement, leurs campagnes de publicité offrent toujours l'inspiration idéale : des photos somptueuses de femmes sublimes dans de superbes vêtements. Avec Victoria's Secret, la séduction n'a pas de limites.

Chez Firstborn, chaque fois que nous abordons le design d'une nouvelle interface, nous réfléchissons à une solution graphique qui puisse se transformer en accroche interactive. Pour le moment, nous avons travaillé sur trois grands lancements. Victoria's Secret : Blue London Jean en 2003, IPEX™ en 2005 et le 10ème anniversaire de la collection de maillots de bain en 2005. Pour les trois projets, il fallait créer un mini-site au sein du site de Victoria's Secret. Chaque mini-site devait avoir sa propre atmosphère, qui devait parfaitement traduire le message de la marque d'une façon nouvelle et passionnante. Naturellement, le format du mini-site nous a permis d'être créatifs et d'essayer des concepts et des modes de navigation qui sortaient des sentiers battus.

BLUE-JEAN NUMÉRIQUE. Pour relancer sa collection de jeans, Blue London Jean, Victoria's Secret a chargé Firstborn de créer un site sophistiqué qui renouvellerait la sensualité de la marque tout en donnant des informations pratiques sur les jeans.

Dans ce cas, nous avons tout de suite remarqué que les images fournies par le client (en plus d'être irrésistibles) étaient faciles à transformer en silhouettes. Les silhouettes des mannequins, les unes à côté des autres,

ressemblaient à des lettres. Les lettres et les mots sont la forme de navigation la plus commune, et cette idée nous a conduit à penser que l'on pourrait utiliser les images elles-mêmes pour naviguer sur le site.

Nous avons aussi intégré le mécanisme de la ligne verticale qui suit la souris et qui définit la limite du masque qui cache une partie de l'image. Ainsi, tous les mannequins étaient toujours visibles, et l'image agrandie n'en était que plus intrigante. Cela produisait également un effet de « révélation » intéressant. Avec un simple mouvement de souris, les utilisateurs pouvaient voir des vues détaillées des huit styles de jeans et des douze couleurs.

Après avoir obtenu une idée raisonnablement claire de l'accroche interactive du « Style Index », nous avons commencé à réfléchir à la variation que nous allions lui appliquer pour la page « Style Detail ». Nous avons décidé de mettre la ligne de « révélation » à l'horizontale. Le masque révélait ainsi un agrandissement de l'un des mannequins.

Nous avons appliqué la même logique à l'autre moitié du site : les pages « Wash Index » et « Wash Detail ». En ajoutant partout dans le site des liens menant aux autres parties du site, tout le contenu était accessible depuis n'importe quel point. Pour compléter la symétrie à quatre parties du site, nous avons placé le logo « Blue London Jean » dans quatre quarts de cercle différents, accentuant l'équilibre de la structure.

Des lignes féminines, des courbes sensuelles, des coupes parfaites pour de nombreuses formes et de nombreuses tailles, douze couleurs, huit styles. Une collection de jeans sexy présentée sur un support

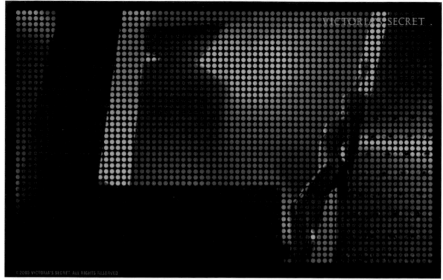

numérique.

Le site Blue London Jean, innovant et instructif, sexy et simple à utiliser, a été un début numérique prometteur pour la collection de jeans de Victoria's Secret.

LA RÉVOLUTION SEXY. Qui a dit que la technologie ne pouvait pas être sexy, sensuelle, ou même un atout de poids pour un nouveau soutien-gorge ? L'année 2005 a commencé par l'arrivée d'un soutien-gorge révolutionnaire, baptisé IPEX™. Si vous êtes curieux de savoir de quoi il s'agit, c'est un soutien-gorge poids plume qui utilise le dernier cri en matière de technologie numérique et laser.

Pour le lancement du soutien-gorge le plus sophistiqué du monde, Firstborn devait créer tout un monde interactif en Flash pour raconter l'histoire de l'IPEX™.

Bien sûr, la top model Gisele Bundchen nous a un peu aidés. Cette fois encore, pour l'interface nous nous sommes inspirés de la silhouette du mannequin photographiée sur fond noir, mais nous sommes allés plus loin et nous avons imaginé toute une galaxie composée de constellations de Gisele... Et où que vous vouliez aller dans cette galaxie, il fallait voyager à travers l'espace nébuleux. Tout cela traduit en Flash donnait l'impression d'un ultrazoom qui vous faisait voler devant des images de Gisele dans l'espace sidéral.

Le projet IPEX™ comprenait deux phases : le premier lancement en mars, et un deuxième lancement en août, sur une échelle beaucoup plus petite. Pour le deuxième projet IPEX™, nous nous sommes inspirés des publicités pleines d'énergie que Victoria's Secret avait produites.

On y voyait des mannequins qui dansaient sur une scène devant un immense logo IPEX™. La séquence d'introduction utilisait une texture maillée pour illustrer une séduction haute technologie, et les transitions étaient représentées par un spot décrivant des cercles sur la scène. Nous voulions un univers théâtral qui projetterait assez d'énergie et de séduction dans le message de la marque.

Le lancement du soutien-gorge IPEX™, accompagné par de grandes affiches, des spots télé et des doubles pages de magazines, a été un grand succès pour Victoria's Secret. Cette campagne interactive a éduqué le consommateur et a souligné l'importance de la technologie pour la marque.

10 ANS DE SÉDUCTION. 2005 était l'année du 10ème anniversaire de la collection de maillots de bain de Victoria's Secret. Pour célébrer une décennie de succès, de style et de séduction, Victoria's Secret a organisé un événement télévisé et a publié un livre exclusif, SEXY, présentant les œuvres de trois photographes qui ont capturé l'essence de la collection. Après l'émission, Firstborn a créé un mini-site anniversaire. On y trouvait des séquences exclusives des coulisses de la séance de photos, des photos de la fête ainsi que des articles pour la presse et le public.

Au début, nous avions pensé créer une atmosphère sexy, ludique et ensoleillée, mais finalement il nous fallait quelque chose de plus séducteur, plus sensuel et plus suggestif. Les photographies que l'on nous avait données pour le projet dépassaient nos attentes les plus folles, alors nous nous sommes concentrés sur la création d'une galerie de photos mémorable. Les photos étaient déjà inoubliables, mais nous voulions que leur présentation le soit aussi. Les utilisateurs pouvaient prévisualiser n'importe quelle photo en plaçant le curseur sur le numéro correspondant et voir apparaître une miniature en haut à droite ou en bas à gauche de la photo actuelle, selon la position du numéro dans la ligne. Cela paraît simple, mais l'effet produit était une navigation basculante inhabituelle, qui a facilement été adaptée à la galerie vidéo, et qui rendait la visite plus intéressante que s'il s'était simplement agi de cliquer de façon linéaire.

La campagne en ligne a très bien accompagné l'événement, et a bien transmis l'information au public : la collection de maillots de bain de Victoria's Secret était plus torride que jamais. Les VIP ont reçu un livre spécial célébrant une décennie de superbes maillots de bain et les mannequins qui les ont portés.

Travailler sur ces projets pour Victoria's Secret a vraiment été une expérience très enrichissante du point de vue créatif. La fusion parfaite de notre esthétique avec les superbes matériaux fournis par le client a donné des campagnes en ligne tout à la fois séduisantes et fonctionnelles.

Firstborn est une agence interactive new-yorkaise fondée en 1997. Firstborn a produit des projets primés dans le domaine de l'interaction et de la publication pour des clients prestigieux dans différents secteurs. <www.firstbornmultimedia.com>

"Personally, I just don't like a lot of padding in my bra. I like me. That's why I like this one. It's light, but I don't have to worry about anything showing." - *Supermodel Gisele Bundchen*

EXCLUSIVE VIDEO

21ST CENTURY TECHNOLOGY. 21ST CENTURY SEXY.
Victoria's Secret is proud to introduce a revolutionary advancement in bra technology. Body By Victoria® with IPEX™. Two years in development, IPEX™ is the remarkable achievement of an international collaboration of designers, engineers and technicians using the latest in digital and laser technology and proprietary manufacturing processes.

For years, women have asked for a super lightweight bra that provided the coverage and confidence of fully lined bras. It didn't exist because it couldn't exist. The technology to produce a graduated pad, one that provided coverage at its center, but virtually disappeared towards the edge, simply wasn't available. Until now.

SHOP IPEX
©2005 VICTORIA'S SECRET. ALL RIGHTS RESERVED

IPEX
THE WORLD'S MOST ADVANCED BRA

VICTORIA'S SECRET

THE MOVIE
THE TECHNOLOGY
THE STORY
WHY IT'S GISELE'S FAVORITE BRA

BREAKTHROUGH!
Combining extensive engineering, research and resolve, the Victoria's Secret team created a fusing process that allows us to gradually feather or shave multiple layers of material to form the perfect pad - maximum coverage at the center, virtually weightless at the edges. We call it IPEX™, and have filed for a patent with the United States Government.

We're introducing IPEX™ technology in a new, seamless, micro-smooth Body By Victoria® shell to create a spectacularly advanced bra - comfortable, lightweight, with the confidence of complete coverage.

We invite you to try Body By Victoria® with IPEX™ today. A bra this advanced could only have come from Victoria's Secret. TRY IPEX TODAY.

SHOP IPEX
©2005 VICTORIA'S SECRET. ALL RIGHTS RESERVED

IPEX
PATENT PENDING

THE WORLD'S MOST ADVANCED BRA

VICTORIA'S SECRET

Victoria's Secret Website

Firstborn

SEXY SELLS. Bei einem Kunden wie Victoria's Secret kann man es sich nicht leisten, eine Design-Lösung von der Stange anzubieten – sie muss frisch und unkonventionell sein. Zum Glück sind die Werbekampagnen von Victoria's Secret immer inspirierend – schöne Fotos von schönen Frauen in schönen Kleidern! Dem sexy Look sind keine Grenzen gesetzt.

Bei einem neuen Oberflächendesign überlegen wir bei Firstborn zunächst, welche grafischen Mittel für die interaktive Gestaltung geeignet sind. Bisher haben wir an drei großen Launches für Victoria's Secret gearbeitet: Blue London Jean im Jahr 2003 sowie IPEX® und das 10-jährige Bestehen der Badekollektion 2005. Bei allen Projekten sollte eine Mini-Website gestaltet werden, die in die bestehende Website von Victoria's Secret integriert wurde. Jede Seite musste einen eigenen Charakter aufweisen, der auf persönliche und aufregend neue Weise die Botschaft der Marke vermittelte – natürlich hatten wir auch genügend Raum, um mit unkonventionellen Designs und Navigationen zu experimentieren.

VIRTUELLE JEANS. Um die Jeanskollektion Blue London Jean zu relaunchen, beauftragte Victoria's Secret Firstborn damit, eine Website zu entwerfen, die die Sinnlichkeit der Marke widerspiegeln und zugleich praktische Informationen vermitteln sollte.

Das erste, was uns an den Fotos auffiel (außer, dass sie unwiderstehlich sexy waren), war, dass sie leicht in Silhouetten umgewandelt werden konnten. Wenn die Models in einer Reihe standen, sahen ihre Umrisse wie Buchstaben aus. Überall auf der Welt benutzt man Buchstaben und Wörter, und wir kamen auf die Idee, die Bilder selbst als Hauptelemente der Navigation zu nutzen.

Ein weiteres Element war die vertikale, der Mausbewegung folgende Linie. Sie definierte den Rand der Maske, die einen Teil des Bildes verdeckte. Dadurch konnte man alle Models ganz darstellen und das größere Bild wurde noch faszinierender. Dies führte auch zu einem visuell aufregenden „Enthüllungseffekt", der es ermöglichte, mit einer Mausbewegung Detailansichten der acht Jeans-Styles und zwölf verschiedenen Waschungen zu betrachten.

Nachdem wir den interaktiven Aufbau des „Style Index" ausgearbeitet hatten, wollten wir die „Style Detail"-Seite etwas anders gestalten. So drehten wir das Layout um 90 Grad und legten die „Enthüllungslinie" horizontal an. Dadurch konnte die Maske eine vergrößerte Ansicht eines Models enthüllen.

Dieselbe Logik wandten wir auch auf die „Wash Index"- und „Wash Detail"-Seiten an. Indem wir auf der ganzen Seite Links einfügten, wurde jedes Inhaltselement von jedem Punkt aus erreichbar. Gemäß der vierseitigen Symmetrie der Website platzierten wir das Markenlogo in vier verschiedenen Quadranten, wodurch das strukturelle Gleichgewicht betont wurde.

Feminine Linien, sinnliche Kurven, perfekter Sitz; zwölf Waschungen, acht großartige Styles und eine sexy Jeanskollektion, präsentiert in einem digitalen Medium. Die Website für „Blue London Jean" ist innovativ und informativ, sexy und benutzerfreundlich und verschaffte der Kollektion ein viel versprechendes Online-Debut.

SEXY REVOLUTION. Wer sagt denn, dass Technik nicht sexy, sinnlich oder das Erfolgsrezept für einen neuen BH sein kann? 2005 wurde ein revolutionärer, extra leichter BH mit dem Namen IPEX® eingeführt, der nach

It's a milestone in Victoria's Secret history. And to get in the swim of things, we're taking you behind the scenes at the photo shoots for the most anticipated swimwear catalogues of the year. From exclusive short films created by photographers to images too provocative to print in the catalogue, see what it really takes to heat up the beach. To kick off the event, we're celebrating with an exclusive celebrity party in New York City. And you've got a front row seat.

YEARS

Of

SEXY

ENTER ▶

den neuesten Erkenntnissen der Digital- und Laser-technik entwickelt wurde. Um die Markteinführung des fortschrittlichsten BHs der Welt zu unterstützen, sollte Firstborn eine auf Flash basierende Website gestalten, die die Geschichte des IPEX® erzählte – natürlich mit ein wenig Hilfe von Supermodel Gisele Bündchen. Auch bei diesem Projekt wurde die Gestaltung von den Fotos inspiriert, die vor schwarzem Hintergrund aufgenommen waren. Wir dachten jedoch weiter und stellten uns ein ganzes Universum vor, das nur aus Gisele bestand … und um zu einem beliebigen Punkt zu gelangen, musste man durch das All reisen. Umgesetzt sah das Ganze aus wie ein starker Zoom, der einen an Bildern von Gisele vorbeifliegen ließ.

Das Projekt bestand aus zwei Phasen: dem Launch im März und dem weniger umfangreichen Relaunch im August. Das zweite Design war inspiriert von den ener-giegeladenen Werbespots von Victoria's Secret, in denen Models auf einer Bühne vor einem riesigen IPEX®-Logo tanzten. In der Eingangssequenz illustriert eine netz-artige Struktur den High-Tech-Sexappeal des BHs, und

ein um die Bühne kreisender Schweinwerfer markiert die Übergänge. Wir wollten eine theatralische Darstellung, die Energie und Sexappeal der Marke repräsentierte.

Die Einführung des BHs wurde von Werbeplakaten, Fernseh-Spots und Zeitschriftenanzeigen begleitet und war ein riesiger Erfolg. Die Werbekampagne machte die Marke bekannt und betonte den großen Stellenwert der Technik.

10 YEARS OF SEXY. 2005 war das 10-jährige Jubiläum der Badekollektion von Victoria's Secret. Um ein Jahrzehnt Erfolg, Style und Sexappeal zu würdigen, veranstaltete Victoria's Secret ein großes Event und veröffentlichte ein exklusives Buch mit dem Titel „Sexy"; es enthielt Arbeiten von drei Fotografen, die den Charakter der Kollektion gekonnt einfingen. Nach dieser Veranstaltung erstellte Firstborn eine Mini-Website, auf der exklusives Fotomaterial, aufgenommen hinter den Kulissen des Bademoden-Shootings, ebenso zu finden war wie Fotos von der Party und redaktionelle Inhalte.

Anfangs wollten wir der Seite einen sexy „fun-in-the-sun"-Charakter geben, aber dann entschieden wir

uns doch für eine eher erotische und verführerische
Gestaltung. Die Fotos übertrafen unsere kühnsten
Vorstellungen – und so konzentrierten wir uns auf die
Gestaltung einer einmaligen Fotogalerie. Die Fotos an
sich waren natürlich schon einmalig genug, aber wir
wollten, dass das „Durchblättern" genauso lohnenswert
wäre. Um die Vorschau eines Fotos anzuzeigen, muss
man mit dem Cursor über die entsprechende Zahl fahren:
Oben links oder unten rechts des gerade angezeigten
Fotos erscheint eine Miniaturansicht, je nachdem, ob
man sich in der Zahlenleiste links oder rechts des aktuellen Fotos befindet. Es hört sich einfach an, aber das
Ergebnis war eine ungewöhnliche Navigation, die auch
auf die Videogalerie angewandt werden konnte und mehr
war als nur ein geradliniges Durchklicken.

Die Online-Kampagne unterstützte das Event sehr
wirkungsvoll und ließ alle wissen, dass die Badekollektion von Victoria's Secret heißer denn je war. Viele VIPs
erhielten ein besonderes Buch, das ein Jahrzehnt wun-
derschöner Bademode ebenso würdigte wie die Models.

Die Arbeit an den Projekten für Victoria's Secret
war in kreativer Hinsicht eine sehr dankbare Aufgabe.
Unsere Designästhetik verschmolz nahtlos mit dem
großartigen Material, das uns zur Verfügung gestellt
wurde, wodurch die Online-Kampagnen gleichzeitig
Sexappeal und Funktionalität aufwiesen.

Firstborn ist eine 1997 gegründete Multimedia-Agentur mit Sitz in
New York. Im Laufe der Jahre hat sie viele preisgekrönte Multime-
dia- und Print-Designs für bekannte Kunden aus unterschiedlichen
Branchen entworfen. <www.firstbornmultimedia.com>

BOOK 10 YEARS OF SEXY

VICTORIA'S SECRET

SWIM 10-YEAR ANNIVERSARY   THE BOOK: *SEXY* VOLUME 3   THE FILMS   **THE PARTY**

◀ PREVIOUS   NEXT ▶   01   02   03   04   05   06   07   08   **09**   10   11   12   13   14   15

DOUBLE EXPOSURE

Gisele Bundchen gives a hand to one of the hottest shots in the exhibit

PARTY THE 10 YEARS OF SEXY

Sony ImageStation
David Lai (Hello Design)

ImageStation is Sony's online service for sharing pictures and video clips. Here you can store, organize and share your photos and video clips with family, friends, and people in your club, team, or organization. Organize your photos and video clips into online albums. Albums can be public or private, and offer captioning and custom presentation. Other ImageStation members can comment on your images and submit images for you to include in your albums. These features help you stay in touch with the people that you care about by sharing images and telling stories about the important moments in your life.

Membership opens the door to a full suite of features and tools including:

- Online storage of all your digital pictures.
- Online storage for 15 minutes of video clips.
- Personalized design and arrangement of your pictures in albums.
- Easy sharing of your images with friends and family through albums, eCards, and more.
- Interaction with other ImageStation community members through Guestbooks and email.
- Stay in touch with friends and family with eCards and other tools.
- Create gifts, make prints, send eCards, and reach out to others with your own images.
- Read great stories, tips, and columns in the ImageStation Magazine.
- View thousands of albums and pictures in the public ImageStation Gallery.

For everyone the "perfect" photo is different, and the ImageStation service helps people reach their creative potential. Once their images are uploaded onto the site, members can easily edit, crop, or enhance with special effects and textures, or choose fun and creative templates in multiple styles and categories using ImageStation's free online tools. In addition to being able to order high-quality prints, users can also print their pictures onto personalized mugs, puzzles or even shortbread cookies.

The ImageStation service is one component of Sony's broader vision for a Ubiquitous Value Network, where devices and products can seamlessly access the network and connect with each other at any time, from any place. ImageStation provides a common imaging platform that allows users to share and store images captured from a variety of digital devices, including still cameras, camcorders, personal digital assistants (PDAs) and notebook PCs. Sony's leadership in both hardware and services puts it in the unique position of being able to offer convergence technologies like USB Direct Connect, which allows members to upload pictures and video clips straight from their USB-equipped Handycam® camcorders, Cyber-shot® cameras or new Mavica® cameras with Memory Stick media in just two mouse-clicks.

Hello Design worked together with Sony to design ImageStation with the goal of creating a site that needed to be highly functional, easy to use, as well as reflective of the Sony ImageStation brand. Hello Design re-architected the digital image-sharing site to make image uploading, storage, organization, and sharing easier and more powerful. The design team also developed a new visual language for the site to revitalize the ImageStation brand and as well as developed a visual

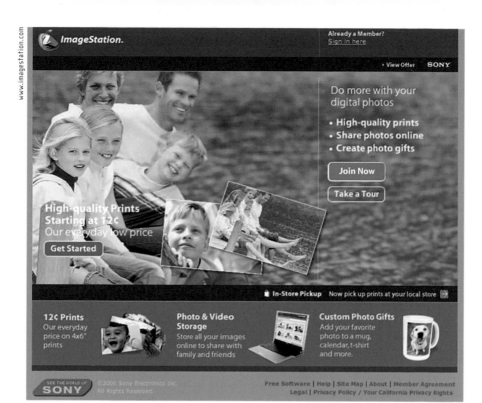

language to attract target demographics including mothers, digital imaging neophytes, and youth. To re-introduce ImageStation to new users, we designed a simple and quick tour to guide visitors through the features and offerings of ImageStation. We selected and used photographic images throughout the tour and the site using imagery that reflect photography and digital imaging in people's lives.

One primary focus of the project was to develop a systematic user interface that would be simple and straightforward so that visitors wouldn't get lost or confused. Main navigation is easy to locate and always accessible. The content is image-driven, using an easy-to-define visual language to indicate items such as albums, products, cameras, etc. Throughout, we made sure the design was pulled together with a cohesive visual structure. Sony also made sure that members have several options to upload their photos quickly and pain-

lessly. Members can drag-n-drop photos right to their web browser, export their photos from iPhoto, or upload complete albums with Sony's free Windows application, ISX. One of the features that sets ImageStation apart from competitors is that it offers powerful customization tools that allow members to create exactly what they want with their photos.

Our team at Hello Design worked extensively to create an easy way for users to order prints and photo gifts through the site. Members can choose from a wide assortment of photo gifts including photo books, flipbooks, bags, mugs, calendars, greeting cards, t-shirts, and even confections! For example, we designed 1-click features for members to quickly access useful tools such as purchasing prints, creating photo gifts, or making photo books. By placing these features in consistent areas in appropriate areas of the site—e.g. an album page—users can make purchases more easily, thereby increasing the site's sales revenue. With new features like In-Store Pickups, members can pick from over 6,000 locations where they can order online and pick up their prints locally to save on shipping charges. Also, by subscribing to Mobile Access, members will have access to all of their ImageStation albums and pictures at their fingertips no matter where they are... all from their mobile phone. Sony ImageStation will continue to innovate to provide enhancements and new product offerings to keep members coming back.

David Lai is the CEO/Creative Director of **Hello Design**, an interaction design studio which he co-founded in Los Angeles. Clients include Sony, USA Network, Oakley, Yahoo!, AIWA, National Geographic, General Mills and Nike. A graduate from Cornell University, David has won numerous awards for his work, and his designs have been featured in Critique, Communication Arts, HOW Design, I.D., eDesign and Print Magazine. As a faculty member at the Art Center College of Design in Pasadena, David taught and lectured on web design. He is also on the Advisory Board of the AIGA Los Angeles. <www.hellodesign.com>

Sony ImageStation
David Lai (Hello Design)

ImageStation est le service en ligne de partage d'images et de clips vidéo de Sony. Là, vous pouvez stocker, organiser et partager vos photos et clips vidéo avec votre famille, vos amis ou les membres de votre club, de votre équipe ou de votre organisation. Organisez vos photos et clips vidéo dans des albums en ligne. Les albums peuvent être publics ou privés, et permettent d'ajouter des légendes et de personnaliser la présentation. Les autres membres d'ImageStation peuvent commenter vos photos, ou vous en soumettre d'autres pour vos albums. Ces fonctions vous aident à rester en contact avec les gens que vous aimez en racontant les moments importants de votre vie grâce à vos photos.

L'adhésion donne accès à l'ensemble des fonctions et des outils du site, dont :

- Le stockage en ligne de toutes vos photos.
- Le stockage en ligne de 15 minutes de clips vidéo.
- La personnalisation de la présentation de vos photos dans les albums.
- Le partage facile de vos photos avec vos amis et votre famille grâce aux albums, des cartes virtuelles et bien plus encore.
- L'interaction avec d'autres membres de la communauté ImageStation à travers des livres d'or et par e-mail.
- Restez en contact avec vos amis et votre famille grâce à des cartes virtuelles et à d'autres instruments.
- Créez des cadeaux, commandez des impressions, envoyez des cartes virtuelles et communiquez grâce à vos propres images.
- Lisez des récits, des conseils et des chroniques dans le magazine ImageStation.

- Feuilletez des milliers d'albums et de photos dans la galerie publique ImageStation.

Chacun a une idée différente de la photo « parfaite », et le service ImageStation aide ses utilisateurs à exploiter leur potentiel créatif. Une fois que leurs images sont téléchargées sur le site, les membres peuvent facilement les modifier, les recadrer ou les améliorer grâce à des effets spéciaux et des textures, ou choisir de nombreux motifs amusants et créatifs grâce aux outils en ligne gratuits d'ImageStation. Les utilisateurs peuvent commander des impressions de grande qualité, mais aussi imprimer leurs photos sur des tasses personnalisées, des puzzles ou même des biscuits sablés.

Le service ImageStation fait partie de la vision globale de Sony, un « réseau omniprésent », auquel les appareils et les produits peuvent accéder et se connecter les uns aux autres n'importe quand et de n'importe où. ImageStation fournit aux utilisateurs une plateforme commune d'imagerie qui leur permet de partager et de stocker des images faites à partir de nombreux appareils numériques, comme les appareils photo, les caméras, les assistants numériques personnels (PDA) et les ordinateurs portables. Leader dans les domaines des appareils et des services, Sony possède un avantage incomparable pour proposer des technologies de convergence comme USB Direct Connect, qui permet aux membres de télécharger des photos et des clips vidéo directement à partir de leurs caméras Handycam® équipées d'un port USB, des appareils photo Cybershot® ou des nouveaux appareils photo Mavica® équipés d'un Memory stick en deux clics de souris.

Hello Design a travaillé avec Sony sur la conception

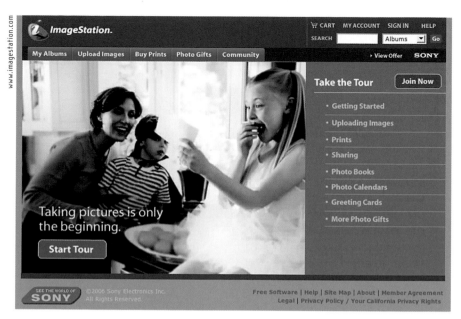

d'ImageStation pour créer un site très fonctionnel et facile à utiliser, et qui devait refléter la marque Sony ImageStation. Hello Design a revu l'architecture du site de partage d'images numériques afin d'augmenter sa fonctionnalité et de faciliter le téléchargement, le stockage, l'organisation et le partage des images. L'équipe de design a également développé un nouveau langage visuel pour le site afin de revitaliser la marque ImageStation et pour attirer certaines cibles comme les mères de famille, les jeunes et les néophytes en matière d'imagerie numérique. Pour présenter ImageStation aux nouveaux utilisateurs, nous avons créé une visite guidée simple et rapide qui explique les fonctions et les possibilités d'ImageStation. Tout au long de la visite guidée et dans tout le site, nous avons sélectionné et utilisé des images qui reflètent la photographie et l'imagerie digitale telle qu'elles sont utilisées dans la vie de tous les jours.

L'un des principaux objectifs du projet était de développer une interface utilisateur systématique simple et directe afin d'éviter toute confusion chez les visiteurs. La navigation principale est facile à localiser et est toujours accessible. Les contenus sont très axés sur l'image, et utilisent un langage visuel facile à définir

pour indiquer les articles comme les albums, les produits, les appareils photo, etc. Nous avons veillé à ce que la structure visuelle soit cohérente tout au long du site. Sony a également veillé à ce que les membres disposent de plusieurs options pour télécharger leurs photos rapidement et sans problème. Les membres peuvent faire glisser leurs photos directement dans la fenêtre de leur explorateur, exporter leurs photos à partir d'iPhoto, ou télécharger des albums complets grâce à l'application Windows gratuite de Sony, ISX. L'une des fonctions qui distinguent ImageStation de ses concurrents est un puissant outil de personnalisation qui permet aux membres de créer exactement ce qu'ils veulent à partir de leurs photos.

Chez Hello Design, notre équipe a beaucoup travaillé pour donner aux utilisateurs un moyen simple de commander des impressions et des cadeaux sur le site. Les membres ont à leur disposition un large assortiment de cadeaux photographiques, dont des albums photo, des carnets à spirale, des sacs, des tasses, des calendriers, des cartes de vœux, des T-shirts et même des sucreries ! Par exemple, les membres peuvent accéder en un clic à des fonctions utiles, comme la commande d'impressions,

la création de cadeaux photographiques, ou la réalisa-
tion d'albums photo. Ces fonctions sont placées dans des
zones appropriées (par exemple dans une page d'album),
et les utilisateurs peuvent faire leurs achats plus
facilement, ce qui augmente le chiffre d'affaires du site.
Avec de nouvelles fonctions comme le retrait en magasin
des impressions commandées sur le site Internet, les
membres ont à leur disposition 6 000 points de retrait,
et peuvent économiser sur les frais d'envoi. De plus, en
s'inscrivant à Mobile Access, les membres auront accès à
tous leurs albums et à toutes leurs photos ImageStation
où qu'ils soient... depuis leur téléphone portable. Sony
ImageStation continuera à innover pour améliorer le site
et proposer de nouveaux produits, afin que les membres
aient toujours envie de revenir.

David Lai est le directeur général/directeur de création de
Hello Design, un studio de design interactif qu'il a cofondé à
Los Angeles. Sony, USA Network, Oakley, Yahoo!, AIWA, National
Geographic, General Mills et Nike comptent parmi ses clients.
Diplômé de Cornell University, David a remporté de nombreux
prix pour son travail, et ses travaux ont été publiés dans Critique,
Communication Arts, HOW Design, I.D., eDesign et Print Magazine.
David est un membre de la faculté de l'Art Center College of Design
de Pasadena, et il y a enseigné le design de sites Web. Il fait
également partie du comité consultatif de l'AIGA de Los Angeles.

Getting Started
ImageStation makes it easy to upload, share, create prints, and much more.

1. Upload   2. Share   3. Create

Uploading Images
Fast, easy and free. There's no charge to store unlimited images and create online albums.

High-quality Prints
Starting at 12¢
Our everyday low price!

Size	Per Print
4" × 6"	$0.12
5" × 7"	$0.79
8" × 10"	$2.69
16" × 20"	$14.99
20" × 30"	$19.99
Wallets (4)	$1.29

Sharing
Sharing pictures and video with friends and family is hassle-free with our online tools

AlbumPrint™ Photo Books
Printed on high-quality glossy paper and professionally bound with your choice of styles.

Photo Calendars
Create custom photo calendars featuring your own images, text and special dates.

Greeting Cards
Feature your favorite image and personalized greeting.

More Photo Gifts
From mousepads to mugs, we've got the right gift for everyone.

Sony ImageStation
David Lai (Hello Design)

ImageStation ist der Online-Service von Sony für die gemeinsame Verwendung von Fotos und Videoclips. Hier kann man seine Bilder und Filme speichern und verwalten und sie Familie, Freunden oder Kollegen zeigen. Fotos und Videoclips können in öffentliche oder private Online-Fotoalben einsortiert werden, die man beschriften und individuell gestalten kann. Mitglieder von ImageStation können sich gegenseitig Bilder zur Verfügung stellen und Kommentare abgeben. Durch diese Features kann man Bilder und Geschichten zu wichtigen Momenten des eigenen Lebens mit Menschen teilen, die einem etwas bedeuten.

Die Mitgliedschaft eröffnet den Zugang zu vielen Features und Tools:

- Online-Speicherung aller Digitalfotos
- Online-Speicherung von Videoclips für 15 Minuten
- Individuelle Gestaltung und Anordnung der Bilder in Fotoalben
- Einfaches Austauschen von Fotos über Fotoalben, E-Cards und mehr
- Kontakt zu anderen Mitgliedern der ImageStation über Gästebücher und E-Mail
- Mit Freunden und Familie über E-Cards und andere Tools in Verbindung bleiben
- Geschenke selbst gestalten, Ausdrucke anfertigen, E-Cards versenden und anderen die eigenen Fotos zur Ansicht zur Verfügung stellen
- Spannende Beiträge, Tipps und Meinungsberichte in der Zeitschrift von ImageStation
- Tausende von Alben und Fotos im öffentlichen Bereich von ImageStation

Unter dem „perfekten" Foto stellt sich jeder etwas anderes vor; der Service von ImageStation hilft dabei, das eigene kreative Potenzial voll auszuschöpfen. Nach dem Upload der Fotos kann man sie bearbeiten, mit diversen Spezialeffekten und Texturen versehen oder lustige und kreative Stilvorlagen aus verschiedenen Kategorien nutzen. Die User können qualitativ hochwertige Ausdrucke bestellen oder ihre Bilder auf Tassen, Puzzle-Spiele und sogar Kekse drucken lassen.

ImageStation ist eine Komponente von Sonys umfassenderer Vision eines „Ubiquitous Value Network", zu dem Geräte und Produkte unbegrenzten Zugang haben und miteinander in Verbindung treten können, jederzeit und überall. ImageStation stellt eine öffentlich zugängliche Plattform dar, die es den Usern ermöglicht, Bilder von digitalen Geräten wie Fotokameras, Camcordern, PDAs und Laptops gemeinsam zu verwenden und zu speichern. Seine Führungsposition hinsichtlich Hardware und Service-Angeboten versetzt Sony in die einmalige Lage, Übertragungsstandards wie USB anbieten zu können, durch die man Bilder und Filme direkt von Handycam®-Camcordern, Cyber-shot®-Kameras oder den neuen Mavica®-Kameras mit Memory Stick mit nur zwei Mausklicks hochladen kann.

Hello Design entwarf für Sony das Design der ImageStation, mit dem Ziel, eine Seite zu gestalten, die funktional, einfach zu bedienen und der Marke ImageStation angemessen ist. Um Upload, Speichern, Verwalten und gemeinsame Nutzung einfacher und effektiver zu machen, erhielt die Website einen neuen Aufbau. Das Design-Team entwickelte außerdem eine neue Bildsprache für die Seite, um die Marke ImageStation neu zu beleben und weitere Zielgruppen wie Mütter, Anfänger

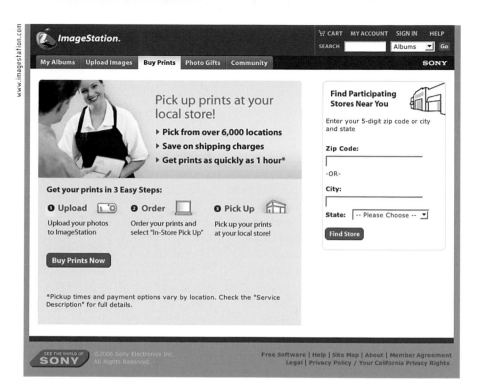

auf dem Gebiet der Digitalfotografie und Jugendliche an-
zusprechen. Um neue User mit der ImageStation vertraut
zu machen, entwarfen wir einen kurzen Einführungsfilm,
der den Besuchern der Seite die Features und Angebote
von ImageStation vorstellt. Um die Einführung und die
Website anschaulich zu gestalten, wählten wir durchweg
Bildmaterial, das die Themen Fotografie und digitale
Bildwelten in engen Bezug zum Alltag setzt.

Ein Hauptanliegen bestand darin, eine Benutzeroberfläche zu entwickeln, die leicht verständlich ist, so dass
die User sich schnell zurechtfinden. Das Hauptnavigati-
onsmenü ist immer erkennbar und zu erreichen. Der Seitenaufbau ist bildhaft und benutzt eindeutige Symbole
für Fotoalben, bestimmte Produkte oder Kameras. Wir
achteten darauf, dass das Design der ganzen Seite ein-
heitlich ist. Es gibt mehrere Möglichkeiten, Bilder schnell
und problemlos hochzuladen: So kann man sie durch Drag
& Drop direkt in den eigenen Internetbrowser ziehen,
Fotos von iPhoto exportieren oder ganze Fotoalben mit

ISX, der kostenlosen Windows-Anwendung von Sony,
hochladen. Zu den Besonderheiten, die ImageStation von
anderen Anbietern unterscheiden, zählen die effektiven
Bearbeitungstools, mit denen die Mitglieder genau das
aus ihren Fotos machen können, was sie möchten.

Das Team von Hello Design arbeitete intensiv an
einem einfachen Online-Bestellservice für Ausdrucke
und Geschenkartikel. Die Mitglieder können aus einer
Vielzahl an Artikeln wählen, darunter Fotobücher,
Daumenkinos, Taschen, Tassen, Kalender, Grußkarten,
T-Shirts und sogar Süßigkeiten! Wir entwarfen
Features, mit denen man durch einen einzigen Mausklick
zu nützlichen Tools wie Bestellung von Ausdrucken,
Gestaltung von Geschenken oder Bildbänden gelangen
kann. Durch die günstige Platzierung dieser Features,
zum Beispiel auf einer Albumseite, können die User
einfacher bestellen, wodurch sich wiederum die
Verkaufseinnahmen der Website erhöhen. Durch neue
Features wie „In-Store Pickups" kann man online bei

über 6.000 Verkaufsstellen bestellen und die Ausdrucke dann persönlich abholen, um Versandkosten zu sparen. Außerdem kann man sich zum „Mobile Access" anmelden und hat dann via Mobiltelefon von jedem Ort aus Zugang zu seinen Fotoalben und Bildern auf ImageStation. Auch in Zukunft wird Sony an der kontinuierlichen Weiterentwicklung und Verbesserung von ImageStation arbeiten, um die Kundenwünsche zu erfüllen.

David Lai ist Kreativdirektor und Mitbegründer von **Hello Design**, einer Multimedia-Designagentur mit Sitz in Los Angeles. Zu den Kunden zählen unter anderem Sony, USA Network, Oakley, Yahoo!, AIWA, National Geographic, General Mills und Nike. David hat seinen Abschluss an der Cornell University gemacht und zahlreiche Auszeichnungen für seine Arbeit erhalten. Seine Design-Entwürfe wurden in Zeitschriften wie Critique, Communication Arts, HOW Design, I.D., eDesign und Print Magazine besprochen. Am Art Center College of Design in Pasadena hielt er Vorlesungen im Bereich Web-Design, außerdem ist er Jurymitglied des AIGA Los Angeles.

The IKEA Retail Websites
HUGE

Think about your last visit to a large retailer. Did you spend time browsing through products that weren't on your shopping list? Did the ideas on display inspire you to think about improving the quality of your daily life?

If you're like most shoppers, the answer to these questions is no. Most likely, you located one or two specific items, and exited the store as quickly as possible. But not if the retailer was IKEA.

THE IKEA EXPERIENCE. Millions of consumers in over 35 markets worldwide know the unique magic of the IKEA store experience. The stores are designed to provide shoppers not just with products and prices, but with knowledge, inspiration, and the joy of discovery. And the IKEA catalogue, of course, is a phenomenon in its own right—a bible of stylish, affordable living.

In short, the IKEA brand is about giving people access to products that improve their life at home at prices everyone can afford. That's powerful.

How do you design an e-commerce site that lives up to those brand values? Our story begins in 2002 when HUGE was asked to design the customer experience for the IKEA retail websites. As IKEA's long-term interactive partner, HUGE was involved in the project from its inception, which allowed us to employ our full research and design methodology

"We started by digging deep into the culture of IKEA shoppers," explains David Skokna, HUGE Creative Director. "Not surprisingly, they had very high expectations for what the website should do. It wouldn't be easy to balance all of their demands in a single design. But we had some ideas."

OVERALL DESIGN GOAL. The first and most important goal would have to be consistency with IKEA's strong brand values. For customers, IKEA is synonymous with functional and well-designed products. The IKEA catalogue and store have a tremendous ability to inspire the customer with lifestyle solutions — to show people that they can afford a more comfortable, enjoyable everyday life at home. The website had to enable a similarly usable and design-oriented brand experience while providing new ways to inspire the customer.

HUGE APPROACH. The project began in 2003 with competitive research and product planning. Other steps included research and persona development, user scenario and feature discovery, tracking analysis, strategic workshops, interaction design, functional specifications, and styleguides.

Throughout the project, HUGE created rapid prototypes of many key aspects of the customer experience, particularly in the area of product configuration and sorting. This enabled early usability testing which informed subsequent design iterations, so that final designs were guaranteed to be accepted by users.

DESIGN HIGHLIGHTS. Key features that contributed to the success of the e-commerce initiative include:

Efficient navigation in the face of thousand of items. IKEA has over 15,000 products. A new product structure and navigation was developed to help customers quickly find the right solution. The solution had to embrace the diverse finding methods customers have developed over years of shopping at IKEA stores and using the IKEA catalogue.

Balance of efficiency vs. discovery. Another big design requirement was to balance the efficiency of

finding specific products with the ability to discover the countless additional solutions IKEA has to offer. HUGE created new ways for the user to access ideas for home living, including the Complete Bedroom guide, which was implemented by IKEA Communications.

Expression of personal style with IKEA designs. IKEA's customers want to create a unique, comfortable home environment that expresses their personal style. To communicate the wide range of IKEA designs, the web-site allows the customer to browse IKEA room settings in a variety of styles, and then get specific information about the products in the rooms.

Ground breaking online customer support. HUGE created an animated chat character in Flash to allow customers to ask natural language questions and get immediate support. The character, "Anna", has several facial expressions that provide additional visual cues to guide the customer through the dialogue. The designer had to create something useful while embodying the unconventional IKEA brand values.

A special e-commerce challenge. Due to logistical constraints IKEA was unable to immediately launch full-scale e-commerce in all markets around the world. In some cases, the job of the designer is to inform the customer in a direct and usable way about the level of e-commerce they could expect.

HUGE TEAM. On a project of this scale, rolling out in over 28 markets and languages, it was essential to create tight interdisciplinary teams. Key players included User Research Analysts, Interaction Designers, Graphic Designers, Art Directors, Animators, and Engineers. Everyone needed to have a close understanding of the strengths and weaknesses of the various technology and design options.

So while we could pick one or two people who worked on this project and pretend that they were the key to its success, we strongly believe the project was successful because of the level of collaboration we set up early on.

We believe there is no better way to ensure success than to make every member of the design team accountable for the quality of the final product. Every designer was given enough responsibility to make it succeed or fail.

RESULTS. The site has become an integral part of the overall IKEA customer experience, and is relied on by hundreds of customers around the world to prepare for their store visits or make purchases online.

HUGE <www.hugeinc.com>. David Skokna (Creative Director); Gene Liebel (Director of User Experience); Aleksandar Sasha Kirovski (Director of Technology); Ann Kristin Persson (Senior Account Manager); Mark Laughlin (Art Director); Anna Arbuckle (Senior Graphic Designer); Kirsten Lawton (Interaction Design Team Lead); Michal Pasternak (Interaction Designer); Monique Saran (User Research Analyst); Billy Fowks (Senior Web Developer); Chris Kim (Web Developer); Fabio Mastroianni (Project Manager); Additional design partners: content development and creation of guides such as Complete Bedroom was handled by IKEA Communications, the division of IKEA that also produces the IKEA catalogue. The natural language chat engine for Ask Anna was developed by Artificial Solutions.

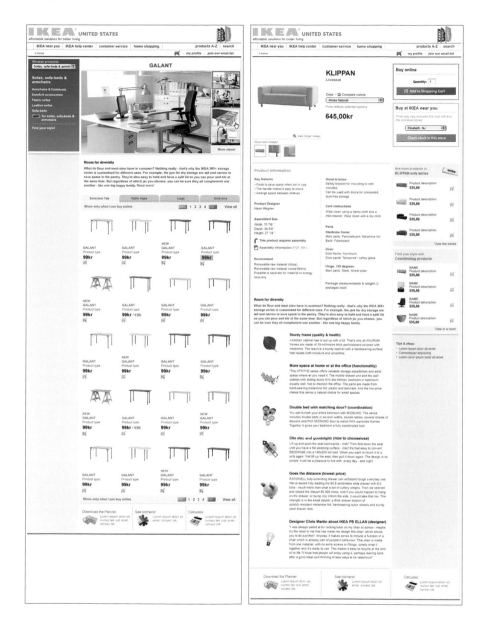

Les sites de vente en ligne d'IKEA
HUGE

Rappelez-vous votre dernière visite dans un grand magasin spécialisé. Avez-vous passé du temps à regarder des produits qui n'étaient pas sur votre liste ? Est-ce que les idées proposées dans les rayons vous ont inspiré des améliorations pour votre vie quotidienne ?

Si vous êtes comme la plupart des acheteurs, la réponse est non. Vous avez probablement repéré les quelques articles que vous cherchiez, puis vous êtes sorti du magasin aussi vite que possible. Mais pas si le magasin était IKEA.

L'EXPÉRIENCE IKEA. Des millions de consommateurs sur plus de 35 marchés dans le monde entier connaissent la magie des magasins IKEA. Ces magasins sont conçus pour proposer non seulement des produits et des prix, mais aussi des connaissances, de l'inspiration et le plaisir de la découverte. Et le catalogue IKEA est un véritable phénomène : une bible de l'élégance à bon prix.

Pour résumer, la marque IKEA donne accès à des produits qui améliorent la vie courante à des prix que tout le monde peut payer. Convaincant.

Comment créer un site d'e-commerce qui soit à la hauteur des valeurs de cette marque ? Notre histoire a commencé en 2002, lorsqu'IKEA a demandé à HUGE de concevoir l'interface client pour ses sites de vente en ligne. HUGE était un partenaire interactif d'IKEA depuis longtemps et a participé au projet depuis son commencement, ce qui nous a permis d'utiliser toute notre méthodologie de recherche et de design.

« Nous avons commencé par étudier la culture des clients d'IKEA en profondeur », explique David Skokna, directeur de création de HUGE. « Ils attendaient beaucoup des fonctions du site, ce n'était pas une surprise. Ça

n'allait pas être facile de prendre en compte toutes leurs demandes d'un coup. Mais nous avions quelques idées. »

L'OBJECTIF GÉNÉRAL. Le tout premier objectif était de rester fidèle aux valeurs de la marque IKEA. Pour les clients, IKEA est synonyme de produits fonctionnels et bien conçus. Le catalogue et le magasin IKEA ont la grande force d'inspirer des solutions aux clients. Ils leur montrent qu'ils peuvent se permettre une vie quotidienne plus confortable et plus agréable. Le site devait transmettre les qualités pratiques et de design de la marque tout en fournissant de nouveaux moyens d'inspirer les clients.

L'APPROCHE HUGE. Le projet a commencé en 2003 par une étude de la concurrence et la planification du produit. Les autres étapes comprenaient la recherche et le développement de l'image, les scénarios d'utilisation et de découverte des fonctions, l'analyse de suivi, les ateliers stratégiques, la conception de l'interactivité, les spécifications fonctionnelles, et les guides de style.

Tout au long du projet, HUGE a créé des prototypes rapides de nombreux aspects essentiels de l'interface client, particulièrement dans le domaine de la configuration et du tri des produits. Cela a permis de tester la facilité d'utilisation très tôt, ce qui a fourni des informations pour les étapes suivantes, et a garanti que le résultat final soit accepté par les utilisateurs.

LES POINTS FORTS. Voici les principaux aspects qui ont contribué au succès de l'initiative d'e-commerce.

Une navigation efficace parmi des milliers d'articles. IKEA a plus de 15 000 produits. Nous avons développé une nouvelle structure et une nouvelle navigation afin d'aider les clients à trouver rapidement

la réponse à leurs besoins. Il fallait aussi reprendre les différentes méthodes de recherche que les clients avaient développées tout au long d'années d'achat dans les magasins IKEA ou d'utilisation du catalogue IKEA.

L'équilibre entre efficacité et découverte. Il fallait permettre aux clients de trouver facilement des produits spécifiques, mais il était également important de leur faire découvrir l'infinité de solutions supplémentaires qu'IKEA peut leur proposer. HUGE a mis à la disposition de l'utilisateur de nouvelles façons de trouver des idées pour sa maison, par exemple le guide de la Chambre, qui a été mis en œuvre par IKEA Communications.

L'expression d'un style personnel avec les produits IKEA. Les clients d'IKEA veulent un intérieur unique et confortable qui exprime leur style personnel. Pour transmettre la diversité des styles IKEA, le site

permet aux clients de parcourir des pièces décorées dans différents styles, puis d'obtenir des informations spécifiques sur les produits présentés.

Un service client en ligne révolutionnaire. HUGE a créé un personnage animé en Flash qui répond immédiatement aux questions que les clients lui posent en langage naturel. Le visage d'« Anna » peut adopter différentes expressions afin de mieux guider le client au cours du dialogue. Le designer devait créer quelque chose d'utile qui représenterait les valeurs d'innovation de la marque IKEA.

Une solution d'e-commerce particulière. En raison de contraintes logistiques, IKEA ne pouvait pas lancer tout de suite un service complet d'e-commerce sur tous les marchés du monde. Dans certains cas, le travail du designer est de dire au client de manière directe et constructive à quel niveau d'e-commerce il peut s'attendre.

L'ÉQUIPE HUGE. Pour un projet de cette échelle, sur plus de 28 marchés et en nombreuses langues, il était essentiel de créer des équipes interdisciplinaires bien ficelées. Les acteurs principaux étaient les analystes de recherches utilisateur, les designers d'interactivité, les designers graphiques, les directeurs artistiques, les animateurs et les ingénieurs. Tout le monde devait avoir une compréhension bien précise des forces et des faiblesses des différentes options technologiques et de design.

Nous aurions pu choisir une ou deux personnes qui ont participé au projet et prétendre que son succès était leur œuvre, mais nous pensons vraiment que c'est le niveau de collaboration que nous avons établi dès le début qui était la clé de la réussite.

Pour garantir le succès, il n'y a pas de meilleur moyen que de rendre chaque membre de l'équipe responsable de la qualité du produit final. Chaque designer avait un niveau de responsabilité suffisant pour décider du succès ou de l'échec du projet.

LES RÉSULTATS. Le site est devenu une partie intégrante de l'offre globale d'IKEA, et des centaines / milliers / dizaines de milliers de clients dans le monde entier l'utilisent pour préparer leur visite au magasin ou pour faire leurs achats en ligne.

HUGE <www.hugeinc.com>. David Skokna (Directeur de création); Gene Liebel (Directeur de l'interface utilisateur); Aleksandar Sasha Kirovski (Directeur technologique); Ann Kristin Persson (Responsable de comptes senior); Mark Laughlin (Directeur artistique); Anna Arbuckle (Designer graphique senior); Kirsten Lawton (Chef de l'équipe de design interactif); Michal Pasternak (Designer d'interactivité); Monique Saran (Analyste des recherches utilisateur); Billy Fowks (Développeur Internet senior); Chris Kim (Développeur Internet); Fabio Mastroianni (Chef de projet); Les autres partenaires: Le développement des contenus et la création des guides (comme le Guide de la Chambre) ont été réalisés par IKEA Communications, le service d'IKEA qui produit également le catalogue IKEA. Le moteur de conversation en langage naturel Demandez Anna a été développé par Artificial Solutions.

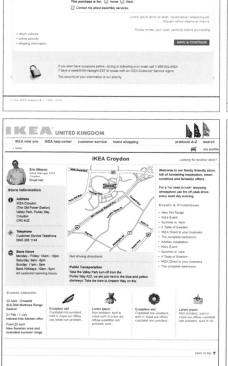

Die IKEA-Webseiten
HUGE

Denken Sie an Ihren letzten Besuch bei einem Einzelhändler. Haben Sie sich auch Produkte angesehen, die nicht auf Ihrer Einkaufsliste standen? Haben die Ideen in den Auslagen Sie dazu inspiriert, Ihre Lebensqualität zu verbessern?

Wenn es Ihnen geht wie den meisten Käufern, lautet die Antwort auf diese Fragen Nein. Wahrscheinlich haben Sie ein oder zwei bestimmte Produkte gekauft und das Geschäft so schnell wie möglich verlassen. Aber nicht, wenn es sich bei dem Händler um IKEA handelte.

IKEA – DAS ERLEBNIS. Millionen von Konsumenten in über 35 Ländern kennen die einzigartige Magie eines Einkaufserlebnisses bei IKEA. Die Geschäfte sind so gestaltet, dass sie den Käufern nicht nur Produkte und Preise bieten, sondern auch Wissen, Inspiration und Entdeckungsfreude. Und der IKEA-Katalog ist ein Phänomen für sich – eine Bibel der eleganten, erschwinglichen Wohnkultur.

Kurz gesagt: Die Marke IKEA verschafft Menschen Zugang zu Produkten, die ihr Leben daheim verschönern – zu Preisen, die sich jeder leisten kann. Das ist eine große Leistung.

Wie gestaltet man eine E-Commerce-Seite, die diesen Markenwerten Rechnung trägt? Unsere Geschichte beginnt 2002, als HUGE das Einkaufserlebnis für die IKEA-Webseite gestalten sollte. Als langfristiger, interaktiver Partner war HUGE von Beginn an in das Projekt involviert, wodurch wir unsere gesamte Forschung und Designmethoden einbringen konnten.

"Wir begannen damit, tief in die Kultur von IKEA-Käufern einzutauchen", erklärt David Skokna, Kreativdirektor von HUGE. "Es überraschte uns nicht, dass sie hohe Erwartungen an die Webseite hatten. Es würde nicht einfach sein, alle Forderungen innerhalb eines einzigen Designs auszubalancieren. Aber wir hatten einige Ideen."

ZIELE DES DESIGNS. Das erste und wichtigste Ziel war die Konsistenz mit IKEAs starken Markenwerten. Für Kunden steht IKEA synonym für funktionale und gut designte Produkte. Der IKEA-Katalog und die Geschäfte inspirieren die Kunden auf großartige Weise zu ihrem Lifestyle – sie zeigen ihnen, dass sie sich ein bequemeres, schöneres Leben in ihrem Alltag zu Hause leisten können. Die Webseite musste ein ähnlich benutzerfreundliches und design-orientiertes Markenerlebnis bieten und den Kunden gleichzeitig auf neue Weise inspirieren.

HUGES ANSATZ. Das Projekt begann 2003 mit Marktforschung und Produktplanung. Weitere Schritte bestanden in der Forschung und der Entwicklung von Rollen, Anwenderszenarien und Anwendungen, Kursanalyse, strategischen Workshops, Interaktionsdesign, funktionalen Spezifikationen und Stilratgebern.

Im Laufe des Projekts entwickelte HUGE rasch Prototypen vieler Schlüsselaspekte des Einkaufserlebnisses, besonders im Bereich der Produktkonfiguration und Auswahl. Dadurch war es frühzeitig möglich, die Brauchbarkeit zu testen und dieses Wissen anschließend in weiteren Designs umzusetzen, so dass das fertige Design garantiert die Akzeptanz der Benutzer finden würde.

DESIGN HIGHLIGHTS. Schlüsselanwendungen, die zum Erfolg der E-Commerce-Initiative beitrugen:

Effiziente Navigation innerhalb Tausender Produkte. IKEA verkauft über 15 000 Produkte. Um dem

Kunden zu helfen, schnell das richtige zu finden, wurde eine neue Produktstruktur und Navigation entwickelt.

Sie musste den diversen Suchmethoden Rechnung tragen, die Kunden im Laufe der Jahre beim Einkauf in IKEA-Häusern und bei der Benutzung des Katalogs entwickelt haben.

Ausgleich von Effizienz versus Entdeckung. Ein anderer großer Anspruch an das Design bestand darin, eine Balance zu finden zwischen der Effizienz beim Auffinden bestimmter Produkte und der Möglichkeit, die zahllosen zusätzlichen Ideen, die IKEA bietet, zu entdecken. HUGE schuf neue Möglichkeiten, mit denen der Nutzer Zugang zu den Wohnideen bekam, einschließlich des Ratgebers Complete Bedroom, der von IKEA Communications erstellt worden war.

Mit IKEA-Design den eigenen Stil ausdrücken.

IKEA-Kunden möchten ein einzigartiges, bequemes Zuhause schaffen, das ihren persönlichen Stil ausdrückt. Um die große Bandbreite der IKEA-Designs zu kommunizieren, ermöglicht die Webseite es dem Kunden, sich in IKEA-Räumlichkeiten mit unterschiedlichen Stilen umzusehen und daraufhin spezifische Informationen über die Produkte in den jeweiligen Räumen zu erhalten.

Bahnbrechende Kundenbetreuung online. HUGE entwickelte eine animierte Chat-Figur in Flash, der der Kunde Fragen stellen kann, die sofort beantwortet werden. Diese Figur, "Anna", besitzt mehrere Gesichtsausdrücke, die dem Kunden zusätzliche visuelle Stichworte geben, um ihn durch den Dialog zu führen. Der Designer musste etwas Nützliches entwickeln, das gleichzeitig die unkonventionellen Markenwerte IKEAS verkörperte.

Eine besondere Herausforderung im E-Commerce.

Durch logistische Einschränkungen war es IKEA nicht möglich, sofort einen umfassenden E-Commerce weltweit einzuführen. In manchen Fällen ist es die Aufgabe des Designers, den Kunden direkt über den zu erwartenden Level an E-Commerce zu informieren. **DAS HUGE-TEAM.** Bei einem Projekt dieser Größenordnung – für 28 Länder und Sprachen – war es ausschlaggebend, mit effizienten, interdisziplinären Teams zu arbeiten. Schlüsselrollen spielten hierbei Verbraucherforscher, Interaktionsdesigner, Grafikdesigner, Art-Direktoren, Animatoren und Ingenieure. Jeder musste genau über die Stärken und Schwächen der verschiedenen Techniken und Designmöglichkeiten Bescheid wissen.

Wir könnten nun zwar ein oder zwei Personen auswählen, die an diesem Projekt arbeiteten, und so tun, als seien sie der Schlüssel zum Erfolg gewesen – aber wir glauben fest daran, dass das Projekt deshalb so erfolgreich war, weil die Zusammenarbeit von Beginn an auf einem hohen Level funktioniert hat.

Wir glauben daran, dass es keinen besseren Weg zum Erfolg gibt, als jedes Mitglied des Designteams für die Qualität des Endproduktes verantwortlich zu machen. Jeder Designer hatte genug Verantwortung für Erfolg oder Scheitern.

ERGEBNISSE. Die Seite ist in das Einkaufserlebnis IKEA integriert worden. Tausende von Kunden aus aller Welt verlassen sich auf sie, um sich auf einen Einkauf im Geschäft vorzubereiten oder Produkte online zu erwerben.

HUGE <www.hugeinc.com>. **David Skokna** (Kreativdirektor); **Gene Liebel** (Leiter der User Experience); **Aleksandar Sasha Kirovski** (Technischer Leiter); **Ann Kristin Persson** (Leitende Kundenbetreuerin); **Mark Laughlin** (Art-Direktor); **Anna Arbuckle** (Leitende Grafikdesignerin); **Kirsten Lawton** (Teamleiter Interaktionsdesign); **Michal Pasternak** (Interaktionsdesigner); **Monique Saran** (Verbraucherforscherin); **Billy Fowks** (Leitender Webentwickler); **Chris Kim** (Webentwickler); **Fabio Mastroianni** (Projektmanager); Weitere Designpartner: Inhaltliche Entwicklung und Erstellung von Ratgebern wie Complete Bedroom wurde von IKEA Communications bearbeitet, der Abteilung von IKEA, die auch den IKEA-Katalog produziert. Die Programmierung für den Chat "Ask Anna" wurde von Artificial Solutions entwickelt.

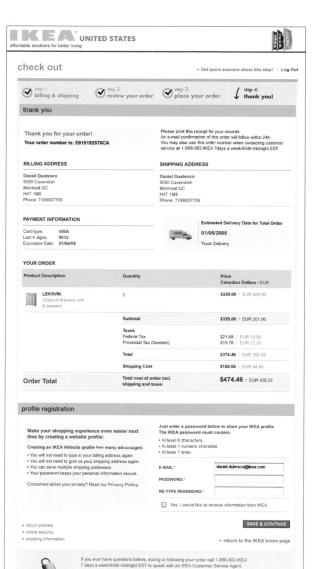

IKEA UNITED STATES
affordable solutions for better living

check out
→ Get quick answers about this step! | Log Out

- ✓ step 1: billing & shipping
- ✓ step 2: review your order
- ✓ step 3: place your order
- ↓ step 4: thank you!

thank you

Thank you for your order!
Your order number is: E015192576CA

Please print this receipt for your records.
An e-mail confirmation of this order will follow within 24h.
You may also use this order number when contacting customer service at 1-888-982-IKEA 7days a week/9AM-midnight EST.

BILLING ADDRESS

Daniel Dustesco
9090 Cavendish
Montreal QC
H4T 1M8
Phone: 7169037709

SHIPPING ADDRESS

Daniel Dustesco
9090 Cavendish
Montreal QC
H4T 1M8
Phone: 7169037709

PAYMENT INFORMATION

Card type: VISA
Last 4 digits: 9012
Expiration Date: 01/06/08

Estimated Delivery Date for Total Order

01/05/2005

Truck Delivery

YOUR ORDER

Product Description	Quantity	Price Canadian Dollars / EUR
LEKSVIK Chest of drawers with 6 drawers	1	$329.00 / EUR 288.00
	Subtotal	$329.00 / EUR 301.00
	Taxes Federal Tax Provincial Tax (Quebec)	$21.68 / EUR 19.56 $15.78 / EUR 12.33
	Total	$374.46 / EUR 356.03
	Shipping Cost	$100.00 / EUR 94.45

Order Total
Total cost of order incl. shipping and taxes
$474.46 / EUR 438.23

profile registration

Make your shopping experience even easier next time by creating a website profile:

Creating an IKEA Website profile has many advantages:
• You will not need to type in your billing address again.
• You will not need to give us your shipping address again.
• You can save multiple shipping addresses.
• Your password keeps your personal information secure.

Concerned about your privacy? Read our Privacy Policy.

Just enter a password below to store your IKEA profile.
The IKEA password must contain:
• At least 6 characters.
• At least 1 numeric character.
• At least 1 letter.

E-MAIL:* `daniel.dutesco@ikea.com`

PASSWORD:*

RE-TYPE PASSWORD:*

☐ Yes, I would like to receive information from IKEA

→ return policies
→ online security
→ shipping information

[SAVE & CONTINUE]

→ return to the IKEA home page

If you ever have questions before, during or following your order call 1-888-932-IKEA 7 days a week/9AM-midnight EST to speak with an IKEA Customer Service Agent.

The security of your information is our priority.

IKEA Help Center

Welcome to IKEA. I'm Anna, IKEA USA's Online Assistant. You can ask me about IKEA and our products and our services. How can I help you today?

[Go]

close

© Inter IKEA Systems B.V. 1999 - 2004

Agent Provocateur
Large Design

One of the most difficult and demanding online challenges is to take on the website of a visionary brand that sets its own standards. Driven by the creative partnership of Joe Corré and Serena Rees, Agent Provocateur is such a brand.

Dripping with sex appeal, Agent Provocateur is an ultra-cool, British brand that empowers women and celebrates femininity. With its' tongue firmly in its' cheek, Agent Provocateur relentlessly questions attitudes and the result is a brand that dictates trends rather than following them. The challenge for Large was to create an online presence that retained this nerve and even pushed the brand experience in what is ultimately a commercial relationship between brand and customer. Like Agent Provocateur's lingerie, the website needed to stimulate, enchant and arouse users but as well as reflecting this brand promise, the website also needed to form an efficient e-commerce platform, drive sales and provide a theme for online marketing activity throughout the year.

Agent Provocateur is consistently listed amongst the coolest brands in the UK, if not the world, and the original Web site launched in 1999 to huge critical and commercial acclaim. Reinventing such an iconic and successful site for such a prestigious brand was no easy undertaking. Large have worked with demanding clients before, including Bang & Olufsen, De Beers and Linn Systems, and knew the very highest standards would be expected so weren't daunted by the task. Over the last decade Large have proved their ability to deliver benchmark projects and knew that if they put the work in and did something original the site would speak for

itself. In the end the creative was the easy part, making sure the whole site had a commercial focus as well as providing a compelling and magical brand experience was the greater challenge.

The concept for the 2005 collection is magic and illusion and Large's job was to migrate this concept online. Large found inspiration from Houdinni, burlesque and Victorian vaudeville and music hall posters. Indeed, the concept of "living, magical posters that have come to life" are central to the development of the entire site. Of course, there had to be a twist, and following, Agent Provocateur's core value of 'empowering femininity' it was vital the girls were in control. Therefore, the beautiful women were not only featured as beautiful assistants but also as the magician, the audience and even the photographer herself. The aim was to create an inspiring voyeuristic, tantalising and playful experience. It's a window to a fantasy world that can become real by buying their lingerie and taking some of the magic of Agent Provocateur home.

The key to any design project is to understand the audience. Large use a sophisticated proprietary process which includes audience profiling, segmentation, user journeys, use cases and wireframes to detail the functionality for every single page - these work as a visual check list for the client and the design team allowing them to think and act like customers rather than marketers. Agent Provocateur's design-led, high-end fashion customers are both male and female and amongst the most discerning in the world. They need to be constantly stimulated, occasionally surprised and of course serviced at the highest possible standards.

Therefore usability and a mechanism for content creation and renewal were as important as a visually stunning site The customer base is also global, so a lot effort has to be made to ensure that the site appealed to customers in the US, Asia and Europe without diminishing the intrinsic Britishness of the brand. The website also needs to appeal to customers who either want to shop quickly or experience the brand and fall in love with the intrinsic beauty of the products.

On order to meet the demands of the customer base, Large decided to go for a best-practice navigation framework to deliver compelling and surprising content but meaning users feel in control throughout. The site successfully delivers some incredibly sharp and visual imagery, animation and video. This was achieved by putting an incredible amount of work into the finish of

the all aspects of the site – the final 1% of effort that it takes to create a truly exceptional site. The photography taken by Emma Summerton was key to the success of the site and the music created by Joe Corré and Luca Mainardi makes the site truly a multi-media experience.

The site is built in a PHP framework with Flash MX used to develop the interactive brand experiences. Large don't use WYSIWYG HTML editors like Dreamweaver and Go Live as they tend to limit the developers' control over the code so the entire site was built using text editors. All the graphic work is done in Photoshop, but a few 3D elements were rendered in LightWave first. The site itself runs on Large's own CMS using PHP and MySQL on a dedicated Linux server.

A project of this size needs 16 weeks to complete from start to finish – the fast moving world of fashion meant

Large were given 12 weeks and with a new collection launching on 1st October an extension was not an option. As the site offers e-commerce, every day the site was delayed would have cost the client money. As the deadline approached the pressure to complete was enormous and at one point Large had virtually every member of the Shoreditch studio, around 20 people, all working on the project from retouching photographs, creating flash movies, compressing video, integrating with the fulfillment company to designing and illustrating the print catalogue.

The result is a site that truly does justice to the Agent Provocateur brand - sexy, original and inspirational.

Large Design Profile. Regular appearances on BBC's 7 O'Clock News, TagesThema on ARD German TV and The Mathew Bannister show on FiveLive has cemented Lars Hemming Jorgensen's position as one of the authorities of his industry. He regularly contributes to the design style magazines Computer Arts, Design Week, Digit, plus adland's journal, Campaign. Lars has controlled countless high profile and extremely successful branding projects. With Jim Boulton, he established Large in 1998, a highly successful Internet consultancy with an uncompromising attitude to quality. Identified by the Financial Times in 2001 as a company to watch, Large's reputation has grown almost entirely through repeat business and the strength of its rapidly expanding, results driven portfolio. Jesper Lycke, Technical Director at Large, has developed a variety of multi-faceted award-winning websites and e-commerce solutions. As technical lead, Jesper runs a set of very capable programmers and interface coders, but is also very valuable for the creative aspect of projects. To complete the team, René Christoffer has consolidated his position as a highly dedicated, award-winning creator and director of intelligent design concepts, across both traditional and new media. He now leads an innovative and creative design team at Large. Rene's field is conceptual and aesthetic design, strategy, brand development and information design. <www.largedesign.com>.

Agent Provocateur
Large Design

L'un des défis les plus difficiles à relever sur Internet est de reprendre le site d'une marque visionnaire qui définit ses propres standards. Agent Provocateur, avec à sa tête l'équipe créative de Joe Corré et Serena Rees, est l'une de ces marques.

Regorgeant de sex-appeal, Agent Provocateur est une marque britannique ultra branchée qui donne le pouvoir aux femmes et célèbre la féminité. Avec une bonne dose d'ironie, Agent Provocateur remet sans cesse les attitudes en question. C'est une marque qui dicte les tendances plutôt que de les suivre. Pour Large, le défi était de créer une présence en ligne qui conserverait cet esprit et qui pousserait plus loin la communication de la marque dans ce qui finalement est une relation commerciale entre la marque et le client. Comme la lingerie d'Agent Provocateur, le site devait stimuler, charmer et séduire les utilisateurs. Mais en plus de refléter la promesse de cette marque, le site devait également être une plateforme d'e-commerce efficace, qui améliorerait les ventes et fournirait un thème pour les activités de marketing en ligne tout au long de l'année.

Agent Provocateur apparaît régulièrement dans les listes des marques les plus branchées du Royaume-Uni, voire du monde, et le site original lancé en 1999 a été un énorme succès critique et commercial. Réinventer un site aussi emblématique pour une marque aussi prestigieuse était une mission pour le moins compliquée. Large avait déjà travaillé avec des clients exigeants, dont Bang & Olufsen, De Beers et Linn Systems. L'équipe savait que l'excellence était la seule option, et n'a pas été intimidée par la tâche. Au cours des 10 dernières années, Large avait prouvé sa capacité à gérer des projets de référence

et savait qu'en travaillant et en faisant quelque chose d'original, le site parlerait de lui-même. Finalement, c'est la partie créative qui a été la plus facile. Le plus difficile a été de donner au site une orientation commerciale tout en le rendant fascinant et magique.

Le thème de la collection 2005 était la magie et l'illusion, et le travail de Large était de mettre ce concept en ligne. Large s'est inspiré de Houdini, du vaudeville burlesque et victorien et des affiches de music-hall. En fait, le concept d'« affiches magiques qui prennent vie » est au centre du développement de tout le site. Bien sûr, il fallait ajouter à tout cela une touche de malice et, pour respecter la valeur centrale d'Agent Provocateur, le « pouvoir de la féminité », il était vital que les filles aient l'initiative. Les superbes mannequins ne joueraient donc pas seulement le rôle de belle assistante, mais seraient aussi la magicienne, le public et même la photographe. Le but était de titiller le visiteur, et de l'inspirer avec un spectacle exhibitionniste et espiègle. C'est une fenêtre vers un monde fantasmé qui peut devenir réalité en achetant leur lingerie et en faisant entrer un peu de la magie d'Agent Provocateur chez soi.

Pour tout projet de design, le principal est de comprendre le public. Large utilise un procédé maison sophistiqué qui comprend l'analyse du public, la segmentation, les itinéraires utilisateur, les cas d'utilisation et les modèles filaires pour décomposer la fonctionnalité de chaque page : ces outils forment une liste de vérification visuelle pour le client et pour l'équipe de design, et leur permettent de penser et d'agir comme des utilisateurs plutôt que comme des professionnels du marketing. Les clients d'Agent Provocateur, férus de design, de mode et de luxe, sont aussi bien des hommes que des femmes, et sont parmi les plus exigeants au monde. Il faut les stimuler constamment, les surprendre de temps en temps, et bien sûr leur fournir un service du plus haut niveau. La facilité d'utilisation et le mécanisme de création et de renouvellement des contenus étaient donc aussi importants que l'impact visuel du site.

La clientèle étant internationale, Large a également beaucoup travaillé pour que le site séduise aussi bien les clients des États-Unis, d'Asie et d'Europe sans pour autant diminuer le caractère britannique de la marque. Le site devait aussi séduire les clients pressés de faire leurs achats ou désireux de connaître la marque, et les faire tomber sous le charme de la beauté des produits.

Afin de satisfaire les demandes de la clientèle régulière, Large a choisi une structure de navigation éprouvée qui révèle des contenus fascinants et surprenants, mais qui laisse les commandes aux utilisateurs. La définition et la qualité visuelle des images, des animations et des vidéos du site sont étonnantes. C'est le résultat d'une incroyable somme de travail investie dans la fini-

tion de tous les aspects du site, le dernier 1 % d'efforts nécessaires pour obtenir un site vraiment exceptionnel. Les photographies prises par Emma Summerton ont joué un grand rôle dans le succès du site, et la musique créée par Joe Corré et Luca Mainardi achève de faire du site une véritable expérience multimédia.

Le site est construit en cadres PHP, et Flash MX a été utilisé pour développer l'interactivité. Large n'utilise pas d'éditeurs HTML « WYSIWYG » (qui permet de visualiser le résultat final) comme Dreamweaver et Go Live, car ils tendent à limiter le contrôle que les développeurs ont sur le code. Tout le site a donc été construit dans des éditeurs de texte. Tout le travail de graphisme a été fait dans PhotoShop, mais certains éléments en 3D ont d'abord été travaillés dans LightWave. Le site lui-même fonctionne sur le propre système de gestion de contenus de Large, et utilise des scripts PHP et MySQL sur un serveur Linux dédié.

Un projet de cette taille nécessite 16 semaines. Mais le rythme du monde de la mode n'a donné à Large que 12 semaines, car la nouvelle collection sortait le 1er

CASE·05

octobre et il était impossible de dépasser cette date. Comme le site a une fonction directement commerciale, chaque jour de retard aurait coûté de l'argent au client. À l'approche de la date limite, la pression était énorme et tous les membres du studio de Shoreditch, environ 20 personnes, ont fini par travailler sur le projet, retouchant les photos, créant des films en Flash, compressant des vidéos, et faisant la liaison avec la société de vente pour le design et l'illustration du catalogue imprimé.

Le résultat est un site qui fait vraiment justice à la marque Agent Provocateur : sexy, original et stimulant.

Portrait de **Large Design** : Les apparitions régulières de Lars Hemming Jorgensen aux 7 O'Clock News de la BBC, à TagesThema sur la chaîne allemande ARD, et au Mathew Bannister show de FiveLive ont consolidé sa position en tant que référence dans son secteur. Il contribue régulièrement aux magazines de design Computer Arts, Design Week, Digit, ainsi qu'au journal du monde de la publicité, Campaign. Lars s'est occupé d'une infinité de projets de promotion de marque prestigieux et couronnés de succès. Il a créé Large avec Jim Boulton en 1998, une entreprise de conseil Internet de grande renommée qui met la qualité au-dessus de tout. En 2001, le Financial Times avait identifié Large comme une entreprise à suivre. Sa réputation s'est développée grâce aux clients satisfaits qui revenaient et à la solidité de son portfolio basé sur les résultats, qui s'est rapidement élargi. Jesper Lycke, directeur technique chez Large, a développé de nombreux sites et solutions d'e-commerce récompensés par des prix. Jesper est à la tête d'une équipe très compétente de programmeurs et de codeurs d'interface, mais il est aussi d'une aide précieuse pour les aspects créatifs des projets. Enfin, René Christoffer complète l'équipe. C'est un créateur et directeur de concepts de design intelligent absolument dévoué à son travail, et il a reçu plusieurs prix dans les domaines des nouveaux médias et des médias traditionnels. Il est maintenant à la tête d'une équipe de design innovante et créative chez Large. Le domaine de René, c'est le design conceptuel et esthétique, la stratégie, le développement des marques et l'architecture de l'information. <www.largedesign.com>

www.agentprovocateur.com

Agent Provocateur

search · wishlist · basket

HOME . New Ranges . Classic Ranges . Hosiery . Accessories . Beauty . Club AP . AP Magazine

PRODUCT RANGE - CLICK THUMBNAILS TO VIEW

Bra   Brief   Thong   Suspender   Body

Back to RANGE

ABRACADABRA

Razzie Dazzle in fuchsia French Lace over tangerine satin. This showstopper includes a body to die for, a full cup bra with great projection, matching thong, brief and a deep suspender.

Abracadabra, I want to reach out and ...

CARAMBA
ILLUSION
BUNNY
CALMITY
CARDINI
HAT TRICK
KABARET
RIVOLI
SHAZAM
SPELLBOUND
TALMA
TOP HAT
WONDER SHOW

ORDER CATALOGUE E-VOUCHERS CUSTOMER SERVICES

undercover investigation . ap lingerie . about AP . stores . currency . contact . sitemap . policies

---

PRODUCT RANGE - CLICK THUMBNAILS TO VIEW

Bra   Brief   Thong   Suspender   Body

Back to RANGE

ABRACADABRA - suspender

Colour   Size   Stock availability
               Small   In stock

Orange   Quantity   Item Price
               1   £70.00

Sizeguide

ADD TO WISHLIST   **Add to Basket**

Shop Assistant   CHECK OUT

CARAMBA
ILLUSION
BUNNY
CALMITY
CARDINI
HAT TRICK
KABARET
RIVOLI
SHAZAM
SPELLBOUND
TALMA
TOP HAT
WONDER SHOW

ORDER CATALOGUE E-VOUCHERS CUSTOMER SERVICES

undercover investigation . ap lingerie . about AP . stores . currency . contact . sitemap . policies

---

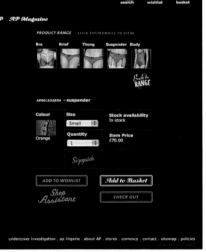

Agent Provocateur
Large Design

Eine der schwierigsten und anspruchsvollsten Herausforderungen im Online-Bereich ist es, die Webseite einer visionären Marke, die eigene Maßstäbe setzt, zu erstellen. Agent Provocateur, von der kreativen Partnerschaft zwischen Joe Corré und Serena Rees angetrieben, ist eine solche Marke.

Agent Provocateur strotzt vor Sexappeal und ist eine ultra-coole britische Marke, die Frauen Macht verleiht und die Weiblichkeit zelebriert. Agent Provocateur stellt mit ironischem Unterton herkömmliche Auffassungen in Frage – das Ergebnis ist eine Marke, die Trends vorschreibt anstatt ihnen zu folgen. Die Herausforderung für Large bestand darin, eine Online-Präsenz zu kreieren, die dies beibehielt und die Darstellung der Marke so weit führte, dass am Ende eine kommerzielle Beziehung zwischen Marke und Kunde entstand. Die Webseite musste genauso stimulierend, verzaubernd und anregend sein wie Agent Provocateurs Damenunterwäsche und somit das Werbeversprechen reflektieren. Gleichzeitig sollte sie eine effiziente E-Commerce-Plattform darstellen, die Verkäufe in die Höhe treiben und das ganze Jahr hindurch ein Thema für das Online-Marketing bieten.

Agent Provocateur zählt dauerhaft zu den coolsten Marken Großbritanniens, und die ursprüngliche Webseite, die 1999 online ging, erhielt kommerziellen Zuspruch und fand Anklang bei den Kritikern. Es war kein einfaches Unterfangen, eine solch ikonische und erfolgreiche Seite neu zu erfinden. Large hatte schon vorher mit anspruchsvollen Kunden gearbeitet – darunter Bang & Olufsen, De Beers und Linn Systems – und wusste, dass man höchste Maßstäbe anlegen musste; daher ließ man

sich von der Aufgabe nicht entmutigen. Im Laufe des letzten Jahrzehnts hat Large die Fähigkeit bewiesen, Projekte zu liefern, die Maßstäbe setzten, und wusste, dass die Seite für sich selbst sprechen würde, wenn sie hart genug arbeiten und die Seite originell gestalten würden. Letztendlich war der kreative Teil die leichteste Aufgabe; die größere Herausforderung bestand darin, sicherzustellen, dass die gesamte Seite einen kommerziellen Fokus hatte und gleichzeitig ein überzeugendes und magisches Markenerlebnis bot.

Das Konzept für die Kollektion 2005 ist Magie und Illusion. Die Aufgabe von Large war es, dieses Konzept online zu transportieren. Sie wurden dabei von Houdini, Burleske und viktorianischem Varieté inspiriert. Das Konzept "lebendige, magische Bilder, die zum Leben erwacht sind" ist zentral für die Entwicklung der gesamten Seite. Natürlich musste es einen Überraschungseffekt geben, und – Agent Provocateurs Kernaussage der "mächtigen Weiblichkeit" folgend – es war entscheidend, dass die Models alles unter Kontrolle hatten. Deshalb wurden die schönen Frauen nicht nur als schöne Assistentinnen, sondern selber als Zauberinnen, Publikum oder sogar Fotografinnen dargestellt. Ziel war es, ein inspirierend voyeuristisches, verlockendes und spielerisches Erlebnis zu schaffen – ein Fenster zu einer Fantasiewelt, die real werden kann, indem man die Wäsche kauft und so etwas vom Zauber Agent Provocateurs mit nach Hause nimmt.

Der Schlüssel zu jedem Designprojekt ist es, das Publikum zu verstehen. Large benutzt einen hoch entwickelten eigenen Prozess, der Kundenprofile, Segmentierung und Benutzerfallbeispiele zur Erläuterung

der Funktionalität für jede einzelne Seite einschließt – diese funktionieren wie eine visuelle Checkliste für Kunden und ermöglichen es dem Designteam, wie Kunden zu denken und zu handeln, nicht wie Verkäufer. Die Die high-end, sehr auf Design fokussierten Modekunden von Agent Provocateur sind männlich und weiblich und gehören zu den anspruchsvollsten der Welt. Sie müssen ständig stimuliert, manchmal überrascht und natürlich nach den höchsten Maßstäben bedient werden.

Daher waren Benutzerfreundlichkeit und ein Mechanismus für die Entwicklung und Erneuerung des Inhalts genauso wichtig wie eine visuell umwerfende Seite. Der Kundenstamm ist zudem global, so dass man versuchen musste, den Geschmack von Kunden aus den USA, Asien und Europa zu treffen, ohne die wesentliche "Britishness" der Marke zu verringern. Die Webseite musste außerdem Kunden ansprechen, die entweder schnell einkaufen oder die Marke erleben und sich in die Schönheit der Produkte verlieben wollen.

Um den Bedürfnissen der Kundschaft zu entsprechen, entschied sich Large für eine optimale Navigations- struktur, um überzeugenden und überraschenden Inhalt zu liefern, aber den Benutzern gleichzeitig das Gefühl zu geben, selber die Kontrolle zu besitzen. Die Seite bietet eine scharfsinnige und visuelle Bilderwelt, Animationen und Videos. Dies erreichte man durch einen großen Arbeitsaufwand bei der Fertigstellung der Seite – bei diesem letzten Prozent an Anstrengung, die den

Ausschlag für die Erstellung einer außergewöhnlichen Seite gibt. Die Fotos von Emma Summerton bilden die Grundlage für den Erfolg der Seite, und die Musik von Joe Corré und Luca Mainardi macht sie zu einem multimedialen Erlebnis.

Die Seite ist mit einer PHP-Struktur mit Flash MX erstellt worden, um ein interaktives Markenerlebnis zu entwickeln. Large benutzt keine WYSIWYG-HTML-Editoren wie Dreamweaver oder Go Live, weil diese die Kontrolle des Entwicklers über den Code einschränken; daher wurde die gesamte Seite mit Texteditoren erstellt. Die grafische Arbeit erfolgte mit Photoshop, aber einige 3D-Elemente wurden zuvor mit LightWave bearbeitet. Die Seite selbst läuft auf Larges eigenem CMS mit PHP und MySQL auf einem Linux-Server.

Für ein Projekt dieser Größe benötigt man für die gesamte Entwicklung 16 Wochen – die schnelllebige Modewelt gab Large nur 12 Wochen Zeit. Da am 1. Oktober eine neue Kollektion eingeführt werden sollte, durfte es keine Aufschiebung geben. Da die Seite E-Commerce anbietet, hätte jeder Tag Verzögerung den Kunden Geld gekostet. Als sich der Abgabetermin näherte, wurde der Zeitdruck enorm, und schließlich arbeiteten praktisch alle Mitarbeiter des Shoreditch Studios, ungefähr 20 Personen, an diesem Projekt und retuschierten Fotos, entwickelten Flash-Filme, komprimierten Videos und waren am Entwurf des gedruckten Katalogs beteiligt.

Das Ergebnis ist eine Webseite, die der Marke Agent Provocateur Rechnung trägt – sie ist sexy, originell und inspirierend.

Large Design Profil. Regelmäßige Erwähnung bei den 7-Uhr-Nachrichten der BBC, den Tagesthemen der ARD und der Mathew Bannister Show auf FiveLive hat Lars Hemming Jorgensen als eine der Autoritäten seiner Branche gefestigt. Er schreibt regelmäßig Beiträge für die Designmagazine Computer Arts, Design Week, Digit, plus adland's journal und Campaign. Er leitete zahlreiche anspruchsvolle und extrem erfolgreiche Werbeprojekte. Mit Jim Boulton etablierte er 1998 Large, eine sehr erfolgreiche Internetberatungsfirma mit einer kompromisslosen Einstellung zu Qualität. 2001 wurde das Unternehmen von der Financial Time als zu beobachten eingestuft, und Larges Ruf wuchs fast ausschließlich durch Kunden, die wiederholt auf die Leistungen von Large zurückgriffen, und die Stärke seines schnell expandierenden, ergebnisorientierten Portfolios. Jesper Lycke, Technischer Direktor von Large, hat eine Vielzahl von vielschichtigen, preisgekrönten Webseiten und E-Commerce-Lösungen geschaffen. Er leitet ein Team von fähigen Programmierern und ist gleichzeitig von großer Wichtigkeit für die kreativen Aspekte von Projekten. Renè Christoffer macht das Team in seiner Position als engagierter, preisgekrönter Entwickler und Leiter intelligenter Designkonzepte traditioneller und neuer Medien komplett. Er leitet bei Large nun ein innovatives und kreatives Designteam. Sein Arbeitsbereich ist konzeptuelles und ästhetisches Design, Markenentwicklung und Informationsdesign. <www.largedesign.com>.

(*Visit the* 𝒜𝒫 *Website*)
CLICK HERE

DUBAI DUBLIN HONG KONG LAS VEGAS
LONDON LOS ANGELES MOSCOW NEW YORK

©2005 **Agent Provocateur** www.agentprovocateur.com

Agent Provocateur
WWW.AGENTPROVOCATEUR.COM

THIS MONTH WE HAVE TEAMED UP WITH
M.A.C COSMETICS TO PRODUCE A VERY
SPECIAL AP TIE SIDE IN AID OF THE
ELTON JOHN AIDS FOUNDATION.

LIMITED EDITION
AP Tie sides

Made from the finest tulle lace, Agent Provocateur's signature tie-side knickers have been redesigned with a pink ribbon pocket for M.A.C lipstick. Flirty and fun, they come in one size only making them fantastic gifts.

This limited edition gift retails at £35 (or equivalent in national currency). All proceeds will be going to the **Elton John Aids Foundation** to support their initiatives in Africa.

To find out more go to the **Charity promotion page inside Club AP**, this online exclusive ends on the 31st of July.

The **Elton John Aids Foundation** is an international non-profit organization funding prevention, education programs and direct patient-care services to people living with or at risk of HIV/AIDS worldwide. The charity was established in 1992 by Sir Elton John, who serves as its Chairman.

Currently ONLY available online. All proceeds will go to the Elton John Aids Foundation.

©2005 **Agent Provocateur** www.agentprovocateur.com

Agent Provocateur
WWW.AGENTPROVOCATEUR.COM

Agent Provocateur

Agent Provocateur

E-commerce Today
Ralf Burghart (Machinas)

Online shops have an enormous potential. Although a percentage of potential customers are still wary of this shopping platform, developments show clearly that e-commerce has a great future.

Customers have understood that online shops can react very fast to their wishes and similarly they can react rapidly to changes in the shop. Competition is, after all, only a few clicks away! If your platform is not user-friendly, it will be avoided.

Online shops are a very easy way of shopping. In an offline store such quick access to price comparisons, concise information about a product or product comparison facilities is not available.

On the other hand online shops need to function like offline stores in certain ways. The client knows his way around as he is used to his surroundings. He enters a shop, a corporate image influences him, he has a look around, considers specific products which he then puts into his shopping basket or not.

Highspeed connections and highly developed product viewing help to counteract the obvious disadvantage of online shops: their virtuality. An honest representation of the product with no distractions or irrelevant details gives the visitor the impression that he will receive what he has ordered and the uncertainty sinks.

Only user friendly websites can be commercially effective and successful. Usability needs to stand out in every detail of the online shop. Therefore we develop shops from the standpoint of the user.

The handling is self-explanatory, the structure of the navigation is simple and the customer finds his way quickly to the product, his aim. Logic and an understandable implementation are paramount.

The core statement of an online shop is a modern design elaborated in the style of the company's corporate image with clear visual communication and intuitive navigation.

The online market is very fast. The website cannot be static. It must constantly be developed and updated to fit the product. Customers who see the same pictures over and over again leave the shop with a bad aftertaste. The customer wants something attractive, innovative and informative. The expectations of the customers reflect on the personality of the internet medium.

The fact that no staff is readily available in a virtual shop must be compensated by simple usability and sufficient information and help. A competent service in and around the shop is a further guarantee of its success.

A good online shop is dependent on several factors, none of which can be left out. The three main questions to ask are: How does the customer come to the shop? How does he find a product? And how does the product reach the customer?

Online shops can generally only subsist through mass visits. The generation of traffic to the site is therefore crucial. All types of traffic generation, be it a banner, newsletter, search engines or offline advertising, must be in the same visual style as the shop. The aim should be to inform the customer simply of what he can expect on the website.

From the homepage, it must be immediately clear how to move on. Gimmicks and tricks are not desired or are not innovations. Nothing must distract the customer from the product and there should not be anything which

has a stronger, more dominant visual impact than the product. The product is being presented, not integrated.

The navigation must be simple. It should represent the product groups of the company. The user must immediately know how to access an overview of the product. An alternative product can also be displayed but at no time should the desire to shop be taken away. Similarities with an offline shop can also be noted: Sometimes customers just want to look around and sometimes they are looking for something specific. An easy navigation through the shop must be available to both types.

If a product awakes his/her interest, the customer will take a closer look at it. The viewing of the product is decisive for the buying. The customer wishes to see adapted images and information relevant to the product or branch. The apparent downside that the customer cannot touch the product must be counteracted by special viewing devices and clear and precise descriptions.

Online shops work simply: Less is often more. The paths are well defined and take the customer quickly to his aim. There should be no dead-ends, the customer must always be able to move on when he wishes to.

An effective, simple and good design is much more than meets the eye. A good-looking shop which does not work is not worth anything. The technology working the shop must function smoothly, with no hinderance and access cannot be limited.

The layout of the page must be quick and reliable. Exaggeratedly big data is hindering.

A successful interplay between design and technique is especially important after the shopping decision has been taken and the product is in the shopping basket.

The shopping basket must come across as serious and make the customer feel secure.

In an online shop the work often starts after the buying as it is crucial that the processing of the order is reliable and serious.

Only when the customer has his product in his hands, is satisfied and returns to the shop can the process be considered as successful. The customer will have gained more confidence in the brand and return again.

The interplay between design and function is measurable in an online shop. The challenge is finding the most optimal way of doing it. Online shops are constantly evolving and a finetuning to the interplay of many different components show the evolution of the shop. Designer egos are not welcome in shops because at the end of the day, the customer is the king.

Machinas offers professional web development worldwide. Experience with customers and knowledge of the cultures and languages in the European, American and Asian markets enable us international implementations. Our service consists of conception, design, development, hosting, marketing, maintenance and analysis as well as e-commerce in special forms.

Machinas takes responsibility for the brand imaging and the corporate identity of international businesses. E-commerce and eBusiness are a part of all businesses. The internet has gained a high acceptance very quickly. A business' brand imaging on the internet is therefore more important than ever.

Machinas services span website planning, design, development, hosting, marketing, consulting, maintenance and analysis. Core to Machinas work is a seamless design perspective with a holistic view of the communication intention and structure for delivery — modern design, clean clear visual communication and intuitive interaction. **<www.machinas.com>**

E-commerce Today
Ralf Burghart (Machinas)

Les boutiques en ligne ont un potentiel énorme. Bien qu'un certain pourcentage de clients se méfie encore de cette forme d'achat, la tendance montre bien que l'e-commerce a un futur radieux.

Les clients ont compris que les boutiques en ligne peuvent réagir très rapidement à leurs souhaits, et qu'eux-mêmes peuvent réagir rapidement aux changements de la boutique. Après tout, les concurrents ne sont qu'à quelques clics de distance ! Si votre plateforme n'est pas conviviale, les clients l'éviteront.

Les boutiques en ligne sont très pratiques. Dans un magasin classique, il est impossible de comparer aussi facilement les prix et les produits ou d'obtenir aussi rapidement les informations essentielles sur un produit.

Certains aspects des boutiques en ligne doivent cependant être similaires à ceux des magasins classiques. Le client sait s'orienter car il est habitué à son environnement. Il entre dans un magasin, est influencé par l'image de l'entreprise, il jette un coup d'œil, examine certains produits, puis décide de les acheter ou non.

Les connexions rapides et les systèmes avancés de présentation du produit aident à compenser le grand défaut des boutiques en ligne : leur virtualité. Une représentation honnête du produit, sans distractions et sans détails superflus donne au visiteur l'impression qu'il recevra ce qu'il a commandé, et ses doutes se dissipent.

Seuls les sites pratiques peuvent être efficaces et avoir un succès commercial. La facilité d'utilisation doit être visible dans chaque détail de la boutique en ligne. C'est pour cela que nous développons nos boutiques du point de vue de l'utilisateur.

Leur maniement est intuitif, la structure de navigation est simple et le client trouve rapidement sa cible, le produit. Une mise en œuvre logique et compréhensible est essentielle.

La principale mission d'une boutique en ligne est de transmettre l'image de l'entreprise grâce à un style moderne, une communication visuelle claire et une navigation intuitive.

Sur Internet, le marché est très rapide. Le site ne peut pas être statique. Il doit être constamment développé et mis à jour pour présenter au mieux le produit. Si les clients voient toujours les mêmes photos, ils quittent la boutique sur une mauvaise impression. Le client veut quelque chose d'attrayant, d'innovant et d'instructif. Ses attentes ont des répercussions sur le support.

Dans une boutique virtuelle, il n'y a pas de vendeurs prêts à aider le client. Il faut compenser ce manque par une aide en ligne complète et facile à utiliser. La qualité du service sera une autre garantie de son succès.

La qualité d'une boutique en ligne dépend de plusieurs facteurs, tous aussi importants les uns que les autres. Les trois grandes questions à se poser sont : comment le client arrive-t-il à la boutique ? Comment trouve-t-il son produit ? Et comment le produit trouve-t-il son client ?

En général, les boutiques en ligne ne peuvent subsister que si elles reçoivent de très nombreuses visites. La génération de trafic vers le site est donc cruciale. Tous les différents instruments de génération de trafic, bannières, bulletins, moteurs de recherche ou publicité ailleurs que sur Internet, doivent avoir le même style visuel que la boutique. L'objectif est simplement d'informer le client de ce à quoi il peut s'attendre sur le site.

Dès que l'on arrive sur la page principale, la suite des événements doit être absolument évidente. Les gadgets et les astuces ne sont pas les bienvenus, et ne sont pas des innovations. Rien ne doit distraire le client du produit, et l'impact visuel du produit doit dominer celui de n'importe quel autre élément du site. Le produit est la vedette, et non un simple élément intégré au reste.

La navigation doit être simple. Elle doit reproduire la structure des produits de l'entreprise. L'utilisateur doit savoir immédiatement comment accéder à un résumé du produit. On peut aussi afficher un produit similaire comme alternative possible, mais il faut prendre garde de ne pas gâcher l'envie d'acheter. On peut également remarquer des similarités avec une boutique classique : parfois les clients veulent juste jeter un coup d'œil, et parfois ils cherchent un article bien particulier. La navigation à travers la boutique doit s'adapter à ces deux types de clients.

Si un produit éveille son intérêt, le client voudra le regarder de plus près. Pour l'achat, la possibilité d'examiner le produit est décisive. Le client veut voir des images et des informations relatives au produit ou à la ligne de produits. Pour compenser l'absence de toucher, les fonctions de visualisation doivent être originales et adaptées, et les descriptions doivent être claires et précises.

Le fonctionnement des boutiques en ligne est simple : la sobriété est de mise. Les itinéraires sont bien définis, et conduisent rapidement vers l'objectif. Il ne doit y avoir aucune impasse. Le client doit toujours pouvoir continuer sa visite.

Un concept efficace et simple fait bien plus qu'il n'en

a l'air. Une belle boutique qui ne fonctionne pas ne vaut pas grand-chose. Les aspects techniques de la boutique doivent fonctionner parfaitement, ne doivent poser aucun obstacle, et l'accès ne doit pas être limité.

La présentation de la page doit être rapide et fiable. Un excès d'information est un obstacle.

L'efficacité de l'interaction entre design et technique est tout particulièrement importante une fois que la décision d'achat a été prise et que le produit se trouve dans le panier.

Le panier d'achats doit avoir une image sérieuse et doit donner au client une impression de sécurité.

Dans une boutique en ligne, le travail commence souvent après l'achat, car le sérieux et la fiabilité du traitement de la commande sont capitaux.

Ce n'est que lorsque le client a reçu son produit, est satisfait et retourne à la boutique, que l'on peut parler de succès. Le client fera davantage confiance à la marque, et reviendra sur le site.

Pour une boutique en ligne, l'interaction entre design et fonction est mesurable. La difficulté est de trouver le point optimum. Les boutiques en ligne évoluent constamment, et la précision de la mise au point de l'interaction entre les nombreux composants montre le degré d'évolution de la boutique. L'ego des designers n'a pas sa place dans les boutiques car, au bout du compte, le client est roi.

Machinas propose des services professionnels de développement Internet dans le monde entier. L'expérience que nous avons acquise auprès de nos clients et notre connaissance des cultures et des langues des marchés européens, américains et asiatiques nous permettent de travailler sur des projets à dimension internationale. Notre service comprend la conception, le graphisme, le développement, l'hébergement, le marketing, l'entretien et l'analyse, ainsi que les formes spéciales d'e-commerce.

Machinas se charge de l'image de marque et de l'identité d'entreprises internationales. L'e-commerce et l'e-business sont une partie intégrante de tous les secteurs. Internet a été très bien accepté en très peu de temps. L'image de marque d'une entreprise sur Internet est donc plus importante que jamais.

Les services proposés par Machinas comprennent la planification, le design, le développement, l'hébergement, le marketing, le conseil, l'entretien et l'analyse. Au cœur du travail de Machinas, on trouve une perspective de design intégré ainsi qu'une vision holistique de la communication et de la structure de livraison : un design moderne, une communication visuelle limpide, et une interaction intuitive. **<www.machinas.com>**

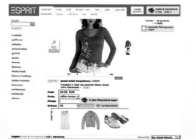

E-commerce Today
Ralf Burghart (Machinas)

Online Shops haben enorme Potentiale. Auch wenn die Berührungsängste der Kunden immer noch sehr ausgeprägt sind, machen die Entwicklungen deutlich, dass der e-commerce eine große Zukunft hat.

Kunden verstehen, dass Online Shops sehr gut auf ihre Wünsche reagieren können, genauso wie Kunden sensibel auf Änderungen des Shops reagieren. Die Konkurrenz ist nur ein paar Klicks entfernt. Wer nicht benutzerfreundlich auftritt, wird schnell gemieden.

Online Shopping ist eine sehr einfache Art einzukaufen. Es ist kaum möglich, in Offline Stores so schnell und übersichtlich Informationen und Preisvergleiche über ein Produkt zu erhalten, bzw. Produkte miteinander zu vergleichen.

Online Shops sollten von der Handhabung ähnlich wie Offline Stores sein. Hier kennt sich der Kunde aus, weil es ein gewohntes Umfeld ist. Er kommt in einen Laden, ein Corporate Image wirkt auf ihn ein, er erhält einen Überblick und sieht sich einzelne Produkte an, die er in den Korb legt oder eben nicht.

Der ‚natürliche' Nachteil von Online Shops, die greifbare Produkte verkaufen, ist die Virtualität. Highspeed Zugänge und weiterentwickelte Produktansichten wirken dem entgegen. Eine ehrliche Darstellung der Produkte ohne Ablenkung und unnötige Details gibt dem Besucher das Gefühl, dass er erhält, was er bestellt und die Unsicherheit sinkt.

Nur benutzerfreundlich umgesetzte Webseiten können kommerziell effektiv und erfolgreich sein. Gute Seiten werden immer erfolgreich sein. Usability in einem Online Shop muss an jeder Stelle gewährleistet sein. Daher entwickeln wir Shops aus Sicht der User.

Die Handhabung ist selbsterklärend, die Struktur der Navigation ist einfach und alle Wege führen den Kunden schnell an die gewünschte Stelle, zum Produkt. Logik und verständliche Umsetzung stehen im Vordergrund.

Die Kernaussage eines Online Shops ist modernes Design, im CI der Unternehmung, mit klarer visueller Kommunikation und intuitiver Handhabung.

Das Online Geschäft ist sehr schnell. Die Seite darf nie stillstehen. Sie wird immer weiterentwickelt, dem Produkt angepasst. Kunden, die zum wiederholten Male das gleiche Bild sehen, verlassen den Shop mit negativem Nachgeschmack. Der Kunde verlangt nach Attraktivität, Innovation und Information. Die Persönlichkeit des Mediums Internet spiegelt sich in den Erwartungen der Kunden wieder.

Nicht vorhandenes Personal in virtuellen Shops wird durch einfache Bedienerführung und ausreichende Information und Hilfen kompensiert. Kompetenter Service in und um den Shop ist ein weiterer Garant für dessen Erfolg.

Ein guter Online Shop ist die Gesamtheit aus einer Reihe funktionierender Faktoren. Jeder einzelne dieser Faktoren ist am wichtigsten, es gibt keine zu vernachlässigenden Komponenten.

Die drei Hauptfragen sind hier: Wie gelangt der Kunde in den Shop? Wie gelangt der Kunde zum Produkt? Wie gelangt das Produkt zum Kunden?

Online Shops leben meist von der Masse. Daher ist das Generieren von Traffic elementar. Jedes Mittel, das hierzu genutzt wird, sei es Banner, Newsletter, Suchmaschinen, Offline Werbung, spricht die gleiche visuelle Sprache wie der Shop. Auch dabei gilt es, dem Kunden

möglichst einfach zu sagen, was ihn erwartet.

Auf der Homepage muss sofort klar werden, wie es weitergeht. Schnick Schnacks sind in Shops unerwünscht, Gimmicks sind keine Innovationen. Keine Elemente sollten vom Produkt ablenken, aber es sollte auch keine geben, die eine stärkere visuelle Wirkung als das Produkt haben. Das Produkt wird präsentiert, nicht integriert.

Die Navigation ist simple und einfach geradeaus. Sie spiegelt die Produktgruppen der Unternehmung wider. Der User sieht sofort, wie er einen Überblick über die Ware erhält. Ihm wird aber auch immer wieder eine Alternative angeboten. Die Lust des Shoppings darf an keiner Stelle genommen werden. Auch hier ist es wieder wie in einem Offline Laden. Manchmal möchten Kunden stöbern, manchmal suchen sie konkret. Für beide gibt es einfache Wege/Navigation durch den Shop.

Ist bei einem Kunden für ein Produkt näheres Interesse geweckt, sieht er es sich an. Die Produktansichten sind kaufentscheidend. Der Kunde möchte je nach Branche/Produkt angepasste Ansichten/Informationen sehen. Verschiedene Tools sind für die Ansicht notwendig. Denn, wie schon zuvor erwähnt, kann der Kunde das Produkt nicht anfassen. Das scheinbare Defizit gleichen besondere Ansichtstools und verständliche Beschreibungen aus.

Online Shops funktionieren simple. Weniger ist oft mehr. Die Wege sind eindeutig und bringen den Kunden schnell zu dem Punkt, zu dem er möchte. Es darf keine Sackgassen für den Kunden geben, er muss immer schnell weiterkommen, wenn er es wünscht.

Effektives, einfaches, gutes Design ist sehr viel mehr, als der User mit seinem Auge sehen kann.

Ein schöner Online Shop, der nicht funktioniert, ist jedoch nichts wert. Die Technik des Shops muss problemlos arbeiten. Zugriffe dürfen nicht eingeschränkt sein.

Der Seitenaufbau ist schnell und zuverlässig. Übertriebene große Dateien sind hinderlich.

Ein erfolgreiches Zusammenspiel zwischen Design und Technik ist nach der Kaufentscheidung im Warenkorb von besonderer Notwendigkeit. Der Warenkorb muss seriös wirken und dem Kunden Sicherheit geben.

Die Arbeit fängt in einem Online Shop oft nach dem Kauf an. Die zuverlässige und seriöse Abwicklung der Bestellung ist ausschlaggebend.

Erst wenn der Kunde sein Produkt zufrieden in den Händen hält und zurück in den Shop geht, ist der Job gut gemacht und ein erneuter Kauf wird von mehr Vertrauen in die Marke gestärkt.

Das Zusammenspiel zwischen Design und Funktion wird in Online Shops messbar. Die Herausforderung ist, hier den optimalen Weg zu finden. Meist sind Online Shops in ständiger Bewegung und das Zusammenspiel vieler völlig verschiedener Komponenten, die im Feintuning die Evolution des Shops darstellen.

Designer Egos sind in Shops unerwünscht, denn am Ende entscheidet immer der Kunde.

Machinas liefert professionelle Web Entwicklungen weltweit. Mit Erfahrungen und Kunden in europäischen, amerikanischen und asiatischen Märkten, der Vertrautheit mit deren Kulturen und Sprachen und eine offene Einstellung, geben uns die Fähigkeit zu internationalen Umsetzungen. Unser Service umfasst neben Konzeption, Design, Entwicklung, Hosting, Marketing, Wartung und Analyse auch in besonderer Weise den e-commerce.

Machinas zeigt sich verantwortlich für die Markenbildung und die Corporate Identity von internationalen Businesses. e-commerce und eBusiness wird heute in fast allen Unternehmungen mit eingeschlossen. Der Kanal Internet hat schnell hohe Akzeptanz generiert. Das Marken-Image im Internet wird dadurch wichtiger denn je.

Machinas ist ein internationales Team, das professionelle Web Entwicklungen für weltweite Kunden entwickelt. Unsere Produkte sind individuell auf den Kunden abgestimmt. Unsere Arbeiten erstellen wir aus der Sicht des Users. Jedes unserer Designs stellen wir selbst in Frage und entwickeln ständig von Grund auf. Unsere Jobs verstehen wir als Aufgaben, die wir mit Freude und Leidenschaft erledigen. <**www.machinas.com**>

Canyon Bikes
wysiwyg* software design

Cycle racing is one of the toughest sports. The bikes have to respond to the specific needs of the athletes and have to be very resistant. Plus: Cyclists are fastidious, pay huge attention to detail and are well informed.

Bikes do exist which are not available in shops. What makes the bikes of the Canyon brand special is the fact that you cannot purchase them in a bike store. Test reports in specialist publications show that the quality of the Canyon bikes is much better than others and they are also more affordable. If you are interested in bikes you could browse through the Canyon catalogue. It comes with selected specialist publications once or twice a year. You could also order the catalogue via mail.

Beautiful images are not enough though. Canyon has decided to bring the brand closer to its customers. The medium of choice for a very demanding target group was, of course, a new website. The first question asked during the briefing was: What does this new website need? The solution was easy: The Agency web designers wanted to create a website on which they would like and want to buy a bike.

For such a task, you need more than various lists with bullet points and buttons with "Buy it Now" on them. Much more. In fact, although the upper-end of the scale of bike freaks does pay a close attention to detail, when it comes to online habits, they are just like everybody else; sometimes curious, sometimes lazy.

What made the task even more difficult was the fact that "upper-end bikes" is an expert science on a level with audiophilie or football. But: A real nerd is not necessarily patient - on the contrary. He (or she) has different expectations and needs immediate, direct and yet different ways to find THE bike.

First you need a showroom - not a till. Many online shops try to guide their customers to the till as soon as possible. Canyon intentionally does not do this: Any car retailer who would try to lead his customer to the till as soon as they had entered the showroom would be considered a looser.

Customers and prospective customers need time. Therefore, the design of the information has to allow an easy orientation. The customer must be allowed to browse the site freely without having to make decisions before he is ready and which he is not able to go back on.

Therefore, on <www.canyon.com>, there are many ways to find your favourite bike (which is, without doubt, the best ever - at least at that particular moment). You can look at it as a whole or at specific details. You can compare it with all the other models over features, weight and price. Or you can study the geometry of the frame and set your personal measurements and preferences after you have read 40 test reports. Many "specials" about current developments and technology enrich the product information and help build-up a base on which the detailed information can show to advantage.

These steps are vital for the "3-click-online-shopping" because without them, it would be impossible to reach the decision for or against a 6,5-Kilo-carbon fibre racing bike or a Downhill mountain bike with a 145 mm swept volume on the front gab because the various small or big decisions for or against a particular bike could concern no less than 2500 Euro.

Last but not least: After you have decided on a

particular model it will be adapted to your personal physiognomy via the Perfect Positioning System. This system is integrated into the shopping process so the customer is lead to a binding order in 3 steps. He receives it via email in a printable format. On completion of the order the customer receives a photo of his chosen model for his desktop.

The concept of the website reflects the concept of the brand. Canyon chose the product presentation concept with their own portfolio: few, but perfect frame forms generally in one colour. These are available at Canyon in 3 or 4 design lines with gearshifts and weight classes. Competitors happily charge double the amount. The website makes use of this principle: Only the possibilities which are actually useful are presented online, instead of many functions, therefore allowing Canyon to distinguish itself from its competitors.

The success in numbers: 30 % rise. The re-launch of the website lead to a trebling of the online turnover, to a rise in the share of online orders within the overall turnover from 20 % to 58 % and also a rise of the overall turnover by approx. 30 %.

The number of deficient orders was reduced by 30 %. Inquiries were reduced by 21 %. The quality of the hotline customer service was drastically improved; most of the questions cyclists asked were answered in the FAQ area of the website and this left the staff more time for more complicated tasks.

According to the results of a representational poll, customers were no longer wary of the possible risks of online shopping on the website, but instead were delighted by the possibility of buying an excellent product at an advantageous price. Three factors are vital: the innovative way of presenting the product, the Perfect Positioning System and the smooth completion of the order.

Technology that cannot be purchased. One downer remains: The current carbon fibre frame of Canyon are so light and stiff that even competitors whose products are three times as expensive cannot top them. Unfortunately, the lightest cycling bike in the world (which actually is useable) – it weighs only 3,8 kilo – can be admired online – but it cannot be purchased. It would not be licensed for the Tour de France anyway. It is too light.

About **wysiwyg* software design**. The agency in Düsseldorf
designs and produces solutions in the new media for brands and
companies. The team which consists of 25 members has won many
awards at both national and international competitions in the last
10 years. It also works for clients such as T-Com, ThyssenKrupp,
Krombacher and 3M. **<www.wysiwyg.de>**

Rennräder Mountainbikes Triathlonbikes Zubehör Bekleidung Service Technologie Über Canyon
Ultimate F10 RoadMaster Passione RoadLite WRX Rahmensets Testberichte

Innovativ. Besser. Direkt.

+49(0)261 40400-10 Fax: +49(0)261 40400-50

Bestellhotline

Bikevergleich

| Rennräder ▾ |

Ultimate F10 Team ▾	Passione Focoso ▾	RoadLite Elite Blue ▾

€ 5.999,00
inkl. Mwst.
zzgl. Versandkosten
€ 191,95 monatlich*

in den warenkorb >>

€ 1.969,00
inkl. Mwst.
zzgl. Versandkosten
€ 63,00 monatlich*

in den warenkorb >>

€ 1.069,00
inkl. Mwst.
zzgl. Versandkosten
€ 34,21 monatlich*

in den warenkorb >>

Canyon New F 10 Ultra High Modulus Carbon	Canyon New F 8 Alu 7005	Canyon New F 3 Alu 7005
Smolik Race SL Vollcarbon	Smolik Race SL Vollcarbon	Iridium Comp Aluminium
FSA Special Edition	FSA Orbit No. 42	Tange Integrated Headset
RECORD 10s Schaltwerk	RECORD 10s Schaltwerk	Shimano Ultegra 10f
Campagnolo Record Compact	Campagnolo Chorus	Shimano Ultegra 10f
Campagnolo Record 10s Ergopower	Campagnolo Chorus 10s Ergopower	Shimano Ultegra 10f STI
Campagnolo Record 10s Ergopower	Campagnolo Chorus 10s Ergopower	Shimano Ultegra 10f STI
Campagnolo Record-D	Campagnolo Chorus-D	Shimano Ultegra
Lightweight by Carbon Sports	Mavic Ksyrium Elite schwarz	Shimano WHR 560
Campagnolo Record 11-23	Campagnolo Chorus 12-25 (bei 53/39) / 13-26 (bei 50/34)	Shimano CS 5600 10f 12-25
Lightweight by Carbon Sports	Mavic Ksyrium Elite schwarz	Shimano WHR 550
Continental Competition Schlauchreifen	Stelvio Evolution	Continental UltraSport
Ergomo Carbon SL	FSA SL-K Mega Exo Monocoque	Shimano Ultegra Compact
53/39	53/39	50/34
Ergomo Power Track Sensor	in Kurbel enthalten	Shimano Ultegra
Syntace F119	Syntace F99	Iridium Pro
Syntace Racelite Carbon 31.8	Syntace Racelite 7075	Iridium Pro
Selle Italia SLR XP	Selle Italia SLR XP	Selle Italia Filante Kevlar
Ritchey Carbon	Thomson Elite (Ritchey Carbon 30€ Aufpreis)	Iridium Ultralight
Auslieferung ohne	Auslieferung ohne	Auslieferung ohne
CarbonFibre Black,MidnightBlue met. oder RaceRed metallic	Apulia red	Classic Italian Blue
54, 56, 58, 60, 62, 64 cm	52, 54, 56, 58, 60, 62, 64 cm	50, 52, 54, 56, 58, 60, 62, 64, 66 cm
6,50 kg	7,70 kg (Compact)	8,80 kg (Compact)

Wählbare abweichende Ausstattung	**Wählbare abweichende Ausstattung**	**Wählbare abweichende Ausstattung**
Campagnolo Record 10f 13-26	FSA SL-K Mega Exo	Shimano Ultegra triple
Campagnolo Record 10f 11-21	50/34	52/39/30
Campagnolo Record 10f 12-23	Campagnolo Chorus 10f 12-25	Shimano 105 10f 12-23
	Campagnolo Chorus 10f 11-23	Shimano 105 10f 12-27
	Campagnolo Chorus 10f 13-26	

Les vélos Canyon
wysiwyg* software design

Le cyclisme est l'un des sports les plus difficiles. Les vélos doivent répondre aux besoins spécifiques des athlètes, et doivent être très résistants. De plus, les cyclistes sont méticuleux, aucun détail ne leur échappe et ils sont très informés.

Des vélos que l'on ne trouve pas en magasin. La particularité des vélos Canyon, c'est que l'on ne peut pas les acheter dans un magasin de vélos. Les tests comparatifs des magazines spécialisés montrent que ces vélos sont d'une qualité bien supérieure à celle des autres marques et qu'en plus, ils sont moins chers. Si les vélos vous intéressent, vous pouvez feuilleter le catalogue Canyon. On le trouve une ou deux fois par an dans certains magazines spécialisés. On peut aussi le commander par la poste.

Les belles photos ne suffisent pas. La marque Canyon a décidé de se rapprocher de ses clients. Pour une cible très exigeante, le meilleur support était bien sûr un nouveau site Internet. La première question qui a été posée lors de la session de briefing était : de quoi a besoin ce nouveau site ? La réponse était claire : les créateurs de l'agence voulaient un site qui leur donnerait envie d'acheter un vélo.

Pour cela, il faut plus qu'une liste à puces avec des boutons proposant d'« acheter maintenant ». Bien plus que ça. En fait, bien que les vrais fanatiques du vélo soient très méticuleux, en ce qui concerne leurs habitudes sur Internet ils sont comme tout le monde : parfois curieux, parfois paresseux.

Ce qui a rendu la tâche encore plus difficile, c'est que les vélos haut de gamme sont un domaine d'experts, que l'on pourrait comparer à l'audiophilie ou au football.

Mais un vrai passionné n'est pas forcément patient, au contraire. Il (ou elle) a des attentes différentes et a besoin d'un moyen immédiat, direct et en même temps original de trouver LE vélo.

Il faut avant tout une vitrine, pas une caisse enregistreuse. De nombreuses boutiques en ligne essaient d'orienter leurs clients vers la caisse aussi vite que possible. Canyon fait délibérément tout le contraire. Si un concessionnaire de voitures essayait de faire passer son client à la caisse dès son entrée dans la salle d'exposition, il serait considéré un bien piètre vendeur.

Les clients et les prospects ont besoin de temps. La structure de l'information doit donc faciliter leur orientation. Le client doit pouvoir naviguer librement sur le site sans devoir prendre de décision prématurée ou irréversible.

C'est pourquoi <www.canyon.com> propose de nombreux moyens de trouver votre vélo préféré (qui sera sans aucun doute le meilleur de tous les temps, du moins à ce moment précis). Vous pouvez le voir dans son ensemble, ou en étudier les détails. Vous pouvez comparer ses équipements, son poids et son prix avec tous les autres modèles. Ou bien vous pouvez étudier la géométrie du cadre et indiquer vos mesures et vos préférences après avoir lu 40 rapports d'essais. L'information sur le produit est complétée par de nombreux bulletins spéciaux sur les évolutions récentes et sur la technologie actuelle, qui permettent d'établir une base sur laquelle l'information détaillée peut se révéler être un avantage.

Ces étapes sont essentielles pour un « achat en 3 clics », car sans elles il serait impossible de se décider

pour ou contre un vélo de course de 6,5 kilos en carbone ou un vélo de descente avec un amortisseur avant de 145 mm, parce que les différentes décisions à prendre, grandes ou petites, pourraient concerner pas moins de 2 500 euros.

Enfin et surtout, une fois que vous aurez choisi un modèle, le Perfect Positioning System l'adaptera à vos mensurations. Ce système est intégré au processus d'achat afin de conduire le client à une commande ferme en trois étapes. Il la reçoit par e-mail en format imprimable. Lorsqu'il finalise sa commande, le client reçoit une photo du modèle qu'il a choisi à utiliser en fond d'écran.

Le concept du site reflète le concept de la marque. Canyon a choisi la présentation de ses produits à l'image leur propre portfolio : les cadres sont peu nombreux et généralement en une seule couleur, mais ils sont parfaits. Chez Canyon, ils sont disponibles en 3 ou 4 déclinaisons, avec différents changements de vitesse et différentes classes de poids. Les concurrents doublent allègrement les prix. Le site applique ce principe : seules les options vraiment utiles sont présentées, ce qui permet à Canyon de se distinguer de ses concurrents qui proposent une myriade de fonctions.

Le succès en chiffres : une augmentation de 30 %. Le lancement du nouveau site a triplé le chiffre d'affaires de la boutique en ligne. Les commandes en ligne représentent maintenant 58 % du total au lieu de 20 %, et le chiffre d'affaires total a augmenté d'environ 30 %.

Le nombre de commandes incorrectes a baissé de 30 %. Les demandes d'information ont baissé de 21 %. La qualité de la ligne de service client s'est considérablement améliorée. Les réponses à la plupart des questions que les cyclistes posaient se trouvent maintenant sur la page « questions fréquentes », ce qui laisse à l'équipe plus de temps pour s'occuper de tâches plus compliquées.

D'après les résultats d'un sondage représentatif, les clients ne sont plus rebutés par les risques potentiels de l'achat en ligne, et sont enchantés de pouvoir acheter un produit excellent à un prix avantageux. Trois facteurs sont essentiels : la présentation innovante du produit, le Perfect Positioning System, et la fluidité du processus d'achat.

Une technologie qui ne s'achète pas. Mais il reste un point noir. Actuellement, les cadres en carbone de Canyon sont si légers et si rigides que même les concurrents dont les produits sont trois fois plus chers n'arrivent pas à faire mieux. Malheureusement, le vélo le plus léger du monde (et utilisable), qui ne pèse que 3,8 kilos, peut être admiré sur le site mais il est impossible de l'acheter. De toute façon, ce vélo ne serait pas autorisé à courir le Tour de France. Il est trop léger.

À propos de **wysiwyg* software design**. Située à Düsseldorf, l'agence conçoit et produit des solutions dans le domaine des nouveaux médias pour des marques et des entreprises. L'équipe, composée de 25 membres, a reçu de nombreuses récompenses lors de compétitions nationales et internationales au cours des 10 dernières années. Elle travaille pour des clients tels que T-Com, ThyssenKrupp, Krombacher et 3M. <**www.wysiwyg.de**>

canyon

Innovativ. Besser. Direkt.

Rennräder **Mountainbikes** Triathlonbikes Zubehör Bekleidung Service Technologie Über Canyon
Torque Nerve ESX / ES Spectral Nerve XC Nerve RC WXC **Hardtails** Rahmensets Testberichte
GrandCanyon Ltd GrandCanyon Ultimate GrandCanyon Pro **GrandCanyon Elite** GrandCanyon Comp
YellowStone SandStone BigBear Iowa GrandMesa

+49(0)261 40400-10 Fax: +49(0)261 40400-50
Bestellhotline

🔍 zoom

GrandCanyon Elite

€ 1.499,00 inkl. Mwst.
zzgl. Versandkosten
€ 47,96 monatlich*

in den warenkorb »

Warenkorb

noch leer.

Marathon   XC/Tour   All Mountain   Enduro   Freeride   Downhill

Bikevergleich
Vergleichen Sie verschiedene Canyon Modelle.

❶ ❷ ❸

highlights   ausstattung   geometrie   **technologie**

HT Race Series

🖨 Druckversion

✉ Tell a friend

DE MARCHI

Canyon proudly presents:
De Marchi Bikewear jetzt
endlich auch in Deutschland.

Die „Best Bikes"-Wahl 2005 im Mountainbike Magazin: Das Yellowstone und
das Grand Canyon Pro gewinnen wie auch bereits 2004 jeweils ihre
Kategorie bei der populärsten Leserwahl Deutschlands. Das sind zwei von
drei möglichen Siegen in den wichtigsten HardTail-Preissegmenten. Dafür
möchten wir uns bedanken. Die ungeheuer positive Resonanz ist Beweis
dafür, dass es gelungen ist, echte Spaßmaschinen zu entwickeln.
Niedrigstes Gewicht bei maximaler Funktion und Zuverlässigkeit waren die
Vorgaben für die Canyon Race Series. Präzises Handling und hoch
effektive Kraftübertragung machen diese Bikes unübertroffen wendig und
schnell. Intelligente Details, wie die neuen gewichtsoptimierten
Ausfallenden, die schmutzgeschützte Zugverlegung entlang dem Oberrohr
und das semi-integrated Steuerrohr oder das Hollowtech Tretlager in der
Race Series zeigen Klasse in allen Details. Erfolgreiches noch besser
machen. Die neuen Rahmenmodelle sind komplett überarbeitet und noch
steifer und schöner geworden. Canyon HardTail 2006: Eine Erfolgsstory
geht in die Verlängerung.

Testberichte

Was sagen die Experten
über Canyon?
Aktuelle Testberichte. »

Neue 3D-Ausfallenden für weiter verbesserte Rahmensteifigkeit. Das
Schaltauge ist austauschbar.

Das neue Canyon Logo ist ausdrucksstark in den Hinterbau integriert.

Liebe zum Detail. Durchdachte Kabelführung und sauber geschuppte
Schweißnähte sorgen für eine perfekte Optik.

Besonders stressbelastete Rahmenteile werden von Canyon mit speziell
dafür berechneten Konstruktionselementen entsprechend widerstandsfähig
konstruiert.

* bei Finanzierung mit 36 Monaten Laufzeit (= 9,90 % effekt. Jahreszins)

Kontakt : Allgemeine Geschäftsbedingungen : Versandbedingungen : Impressum : © Canyon Bikes 2005   international » »

Canyon Bikes
wysiwyg* software design

Radsport ist eine der härtesten Sportarten überhaupt. Die Räder müssen den spezifischen Bedürfnissen der Athleten entsprechen und gewaltigen Belastungen standhalten können. Und: Radsportler sind wählerisch, detailverliebt und außerordentlich gut informiert.

Es gibt tatsächlich Räder, die es nicht im Handel gibt. Das Besondere an den Bikes der Marke Canyon ist, daß es diese Räder in keinem Fachgeschäft zu kaufen gibt. In den Testberichten der Fachpresse steht, die Räder von Canyon sind um ein Vielfaches besser und günstiger als alle anderen. Wer sich für die Räder interessierte, konnte den Katalog von Canyon durchblättern, der ein oder zweimal im Jahr lag ausgewählten Fachzeitschriften beilag. Natürlich konnte man diesen Katalog auch bestellen. Per Post.

Schöne Bilder allein machen noch keinen Shop. Canyon entschied sich, die Marke näher zum Kunden zu bringen. Das Mittel der Wahl für eine sehr anspruchsvolle Zielgruppe war, klar, eine neue Website. Die erste Frage im Briefing lautete: Was muß diese neue Website können? Die Lösung war nicht schwer: Die Designer der Agentur wollten einfach genau die Website bauen, auf der sie sich selbst ein Rad kaufen würden.

Dafür braucht man mehr als viele Listen mit Bulletpoints und Bildern, neben denen ein Knopf mit der Aufschrift „Bestellen" zu finden ist. Sehr viel mehr. Denn so Detailversessen die High-End-Fahrradfreaks auch sein mögen, in ihren Online-Gewohnheiten sind sie so wie alle anderen; mal neugierig, mal bequem.

Erschwerend kam hinzu, daß die Materie „Highend Bikes" eine Expertenwissenschaft ist, die es durchaus mit Audiophilie oder Fußball aufnehmen kann. Nur: ein echter Nerd ist deswegen noch lange kein geduldiger Mensch, im Gegenteil. Er (oder sie) hat verschieden dicke Schichten Vorwissen, und braucht sehr direkte, aber ganz unterschiedliche Wege zu „seinem" Bike.

In erster Linie braucht man einen Showroom - und keine Registrierkasse. Viele Online Shops versuchen Kunden möglichst schnell zur Kasse zu leiten. Canyon tut das absichtlich nicht: Denn jeder Autohändler, der seine Kunden unmittelbar nach dem Betreten des Showrooms direkt an den Verkaufstisch bringen wollte, wäre ein Looser.

Kunden und Interessenten brauchen Zeit. Deswegen muß das Informationsdesign eine problemlose Orientierung ermöglichen. Aus der Sicht des Kunden muß das so geschehen, daß er sich auf der gesamten Website frei bewegen kann und ihm nicht ständig Entscheidungen abgenötigt werden, die er gar nicht treffen will und auch nicht umkehren kann.

Deswegen gibt es auf <www.canyon.com> viele Wege, um das jeweilige Lieblingsbike (das unbestritten das beste aller Zeiten ist. Also jedenfalls im Moment gerade.) zu finden. Man kann es ansehen, im Ganzen und en Détail. Man kann es vergleichen - mit allen anderen Modellen, mit deren Ausstattung, deren Gewicht, deren Preis. Oder man kann Rahmengeometrien studieren und seine persönlichen Maße und Vorlieben festlegen, nachdem man vierzig Testberichte gelesen hat. Die vielen Specials über Entwicklungen und Technologie erweitern die reine Produkt-information und bilden somit ein Fundament, auf dem die Detailinformation ihre Wirkung entfalten kann.

Diese Schritte zählen beim „3-Click-Online-Shop-

canyon — Innovativ. Besser. Direkt.

Rennräder Mountainbikes Triathlonbikes Zubehör Bekleidung Service Technologie Über Canyon | +49(0)261 40400-10 Fax: +49(0)261 40400-50
Ultimate F10 RoadMaster Passione RoadLite WRX Rahmensets Testberichte — Bestellhotline

Ultimate F10 Series
Die Zukunft hat begonnen. Der Carbon Ultimate Rahmen überzeugt mit fantastischen Steifigkeitswerten und faszinierendem Design. Mit 75 Punkten Platz 1 der ewigen „Tour" Bestenliste. Jedes Modell wahlweise in einer der drei Farbvarianten lieferbar.
Ultimate F10 Team | Ultimate F10 Limited SL | Ultimate F10 Limited | Ultimate F10 Record | Ultimate F10 Pro SL | Ultimate F10 Pro | Ultimate F10 Elite | Ultimate F10 Race

RoadMaster Series
Die RoadMaster Modelle zeigen, was mit Aluminiumrahmen heute machbar ist. Der RoadMaster F8 Rahmen steht für höchste Steifigkeitswerte und eigenständige Lösungen. Entwickelt mit den Erkenntnissen aus dem hochgelobten Carbon F10.
RoadMaster Ultimate | RoadMaster Pro | RoadMaster Race

Passione Series
Leidenschaft pur. Die Kombination aus modernster Hochleistungstechnologie und Design ist eine Hommage an die großen italienischen Meister. Edelkomponenten gepaart mit einem der überzeugendsten Rahmen am Markt - dafür steht Passione.
Passione Focoso | Passione Elite

RoadLite Series
Mehr Eleganz bei weniger Gewicht. Kontinuierliche Modellpflege und aufwändige Detaillösungen machen den Canyon RoadLite zu einem der begehrtesten Rennrahmen. Hochwertige Premium-Rennräder mit bestem Preis-Leistungs-Verhältnis.
RoadLite Elite Blue | RoadLite Elite Titanium

WRX Series
Keine Kompromisse. Bis ins kleinste Detail orientieren wir uns kompromisslos an den Bedürfnissen der sportlichen Bikerin. Bei der ersten Ausfahrt erleben Sie den Unterschied.
RoadMaster Race WRX | RoadLite WRX

Rahmensets
Der Canyon Rennrahmen– die perfekte Basis für Ihr individuelles Traumrad.
Ultimate F10 Carbon Fibre Black | Ultimate F10 Race Red | Ultimate F10 Midnight Blue | RoadMaster Ultimate | RoadLite Elite

Kontakt | Allgemeine Geschäftsbedingungen | Versandbedingungen | Impressum | © Canyon Bikes 2005 — international >>

ping". Denn ohne sie ist die Entscheidung für oder gegen ein 6,5-Kilo-Kohlefaser-Rennrad oder ein Downhill-Mountainbike mit 145 mm Federweg an der Vordergabel einfach nicht zu treffen. Denn bei den vielen kleinen und großen Entscheidungen für oder gegen ein bestimmtes Rad geht es in der Regel um nicht weniger als 2500 Euro.

Das schönste kommt dann zum Schluss: hat man sich einmal für ein Modell entschieden, wird es über ein PerfectPositioning System optimal an die persönliche Physiognomie angepasst. Dies System ist in den Kaufprozess eingebunden, so dass der Kunde in 3 Schritten zur verbindlichen Bestellung geführt wird. Diese erhält er per Mail und auch direkt in einem druckbaren Format. Da Vorfreude ja bekanntlich die schönste Freude ist erhält der Kunde ein Foto seines Modells für seinen Desktop als Abschluss der Bestellung.

Das Konzept der Website spiegelt das Konzept der Marke. Canyon selbst gab das Konzept der Warenpräsentation mit dem eigenen Produkt-Portfolio vor: wenige, aber perfekte Rahmenformen in meist nur einer Farbe. Diese gibt es jeweils in drei oder vier Austattungslinien mit Schaltungen und Gewichtsklassen bei Canyon, die die Konkurrenz gerne für das Doppelte verkaufen möchte. Dieses Prinzip machte sich die Website zu nutze: Statt einer beliebige hohen Vielzahl an Funktionen werden online nur die Möglichkeiten eingesetzt, die dem Endkunden einen tatsächlichen Nutzen bringen und damit eine Differenzierung zum Wettbewerb erlauben.

Der Erfolg in Zahlen: 30 Prozent mehr. Der Relaunch der Website führte zu einer Verdreifachung der Online Umsätze und zu einer Erhöhung des Anteils der Online Bestellungen vom Gesamtumsatz von 20 % auf 58 % bei einem gleichzeitigem Anstieg des Gesamtumsatzes um ca. 30 %.

Die Quote der Fehlbestellungen wurde um 30 % gesenkt. Serviceanfragen konnten um 21 % reduziert werden. Die Beratungsqualität der Telefon Hotline wurde drastisch verbessert, weil sich seit dem Relaunch viele Detailfragen von Radsportlern in den FAQ Bereichen der Website von selbst klären und den Mitarbeitern im Support so mehr Zeit für die Klärung von ansprcuhsvolleren Sachverhalten bleibt.

Einer repräsentativen Umfrage unter den Endkunden zufolge wird der Kauf über die Website nicht mehr als Risiko wahrgenommen, sondern vielmehr als die zeitgemäße Möglichkeit, ein hervorragendes Produkt zu einem ausgezeichneten Preis zu erwerben. Von entscheidender Bedeutung in diesem Zusammenhang sind folgenden drei Faktoren: die innovative Form der Produktdarstellung, das Perfect Positioning System und die problemlose Abwicklung der Bestellung.

Die Sache mit der Technik, die es nicht zu kaufen gibt. Ein Wermutstropfen bleibt: Die aktuellen Kohlefaserrahmen von Canyon sind so leicht und so steif, daß auch dreimal so teure Konkurrenten nicht an sie heranreichen. Leider kann man das leichteste (wirklich fahrbare) Rennrad der Welt – es wiegt nicht ganz 3,8 Kilo – nur online bei Canyon bestaunen - kaufen kann man es nicht. Aber bei der Tour de France wäre es sowieso nicht zugelassen. Es ist zu leicht.

Über **wysiwyg* software design**. Die Düsseldorfer Agentur entwirft und produziert Lösungen für Marken und Unternehmen in den neuen Medien. Das 25 Mitarbeiter starke Team hat in den letzten zehn Jahren bei nationalen und internationalen Wettbewerben zahlreiche Auszeichnungen gewonnen und arbeitet für Kunden wie T-Com, ThyssenKrupp, Krombacher und 3M. <www.wysiwyg.de>

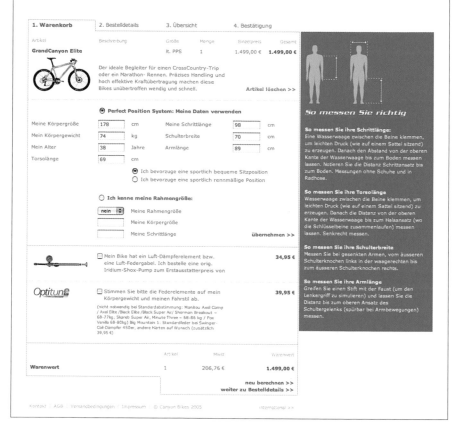

Innovativ. Besser. Direkt.

Rennräder **Mountainbikes** Triathlonbikes Zubehör Bekleidung Service Technologie Über Canyon
Torque Nerve ESX / ES Spectral Nerve XC Nerve RC WXC Hardtails Rahmensets Testberichte

+49(0)261 40400-10 Fax: +49(0)261 40400-50

Bestellhotline

Ihre Bestellung

1. Warenkorb	2. Bestelldetails	3. Übersicht	4. Bestätigung

Artikel	Beschreibung	Größe	Menge	Einzelpreis	Gesamt
GrandCanyon Elite	Der ideale Begleiter für einen CrossCountry-Trip oder ein Marathon- Rennen. Präzises Handling und hoch effektive Kraftübertragung machen diese Bikes unübertroffen wendig und schnell.	lt. PPS	1	1.499,00 €	**1.499,00 €**

Artikel löschen >>

◉ **Perfect Position System: Meine Daten verwenden**

So messen Sie richtig

Meine Körpergröße	178	cm	Meine Schrittlänge	98	cm
Mein Körpergewicht	74	kg	Schulterbreite	70	cm
Mein Alter	38	Jahre	Armlänge	89	cm
Torsolänge	69	cm			

◉ Ich bevorzuge eine sportlich bequeme Sitzposition
○ Ich bevorzuge eine sportlich rennmäßige Position

○ **Ich kenne meine Rahmengröße:**

nein ⇕ Meine Rahmengröße

Meine Körpergröße

Meine Schrittlänge   übernehmen >>

So messen Sie Ihre Schrittlänge:
Eine Wasserwaage zwischen die Beine klemmen, um leichten Druck (wie auf einem Sattel sitzend) zu erzeugen. Danach den Abstand von der oberen Kante der Wasserwaage bis zum Boden messen lassen. Notieren Sie die Distanz Schrittansatz bis zum Boden. Messungen ohne Schuhe und in Radhose.

So messen Sie Ihre Torsolänge
Wasserwaage zwischen die Beine klemmen, um leichten Druck (wie auf einem Sattel sitzend) zu erzeugen. Danach die Distanz von der oberen Kante der Wasserwaage bis zum Halsansatz (wo die Schlüsselbeine zusammenlaufen) messen lassen. Senkrecht messen.

So messen Sie Ihre Schulterbreite
Messen Sie bei gesenkten Armen, vom äusseren Schulterknochen links in der waagerechten bis zum äusseren Schulterknochen rechts.

So messen Sie Ihre Armlänge
Greifen Sie einen Stift mit der Faust (um den Lenkergriff zu simulieren) und lassen Sie die Distanz zum oberen Ansatz des Schultergelenks (spürbar bei Armbewegungen) messen.

☐ Mein Bike hat ein Luft-Dämpferelement bzw. eine Luft-Federgabel. Ich bestelle eine orig. Iridium-Shox-Pump zum Erstausstatterpreis von   34,95 €

Optitune

☐ Stimmen Sie bitte die Federelemente auf mein Körpergewicht und meinen Fahrstil ab.   39,95 €

(nicht notwendig bei Standardabstimmung: Manitou Axel Comp / Axel Elite /Black Elite /Black Super Air/ Sherman Breakout ~ 68-77kg, Skareb Super Air, Minute Three ~ 68-86 kg / Fox Vanilla 68-80kg) Big Mountain 1: Standardfeder bei Swinger-Coil-Dämpfer 450er, andere Härten auf Wunsch (zusätzlich 39,95 €)

	Artikel	Mwst	Warenwert
Warenwert	1	206,76 €	**1.499,00 €**

neu berechnen >>
weiter zu Bestelldetails >>

Kontakt | AGB | Versandbedingungen | Impressum | © Canyon Bikes 2005   International >>

E-COMMERCE · 89

Concept

Actually this is not another image bank, it's a personal photography portfolio ready to sell at low cost some images with the PayPal payment platform.

Info

DESIGN AND PROGRAMMING: Yannick Scordia <www.selfstock.com>. /// TOOLS: Macromedia Flash, Php, MySql. /// CONTENTS: photography. ///
AWARDS: FWA, TINY, plasticpilots, TAXI, Netdiver. /// COST: 100 hours.

Plus qu'une simple banque d'images, c'est un portfolio personnel de photographies que l'on peut acheter à bas prix à travers la plateforme de paiement Paypal. /// Hierbei handelt es sich nicht um eine weitere Bilddatenbank, sondern um ein privates Portfolio mit Fotos, die man zu niedrigen Preisen über die Plattform Paypal kaufen kann.

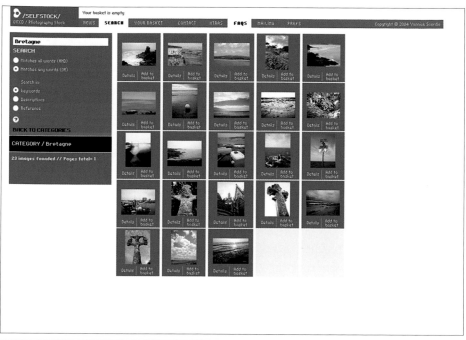

9TO5 SEATING

www.9to5seating.com

Concept

This site is entirely in Flash, presenting the user with a great, cohesive experience. All elements are loaded in dynamically, allowing 9to5 to keep their product catalog up to date without having to sacrifice aesthetics. The site is based on an ecommerce backend, allowing for future expansion.

Info

DESIGN AND PROGRAMMING: Fluidesign <www.fluidesign.com>. /// TOOLS: Macromedia Flash, Adobe Photoshop, HTML, PHP. /// CONTENTS: photos, animation, text, symbols. /// AWARDS: Gold Davey. /// COST: 250 hours.

Cet excellent site entièrement construit en Flash offre un service complet. Le chargement dynamique de tous les éléments permet à 9to5 d'avoir un catalogue de produits à jour sans devoir sacrifier l'esthétique. L'application d'e-commerce sur laquelle le site est basé lui permettra de futures évolutions. /// Die gesamte Seite basiert auf Flash und präsentiert dem Benutzer ein grandioses, in sich geschlossenes Erlebnis. Alle Elemente werden dynamisch geladen, wodurch 9to5 ihren Produktkatalog auf dem neuesten Stand halten können, ohne auf Ästhetik zu verzichten. Die Seite basiert auf einem E-Commerce-Backend und kann fortlaufend ergänzt werden.

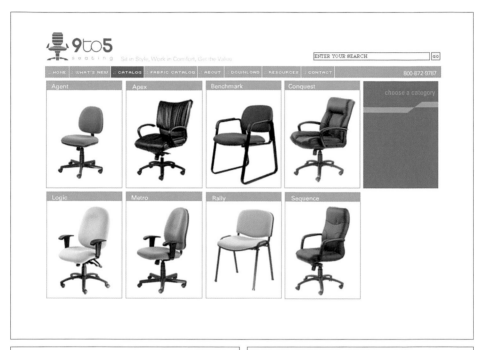

ADVANCE FLASH

PORTUGAL

www.advanceflash.com

2005

Concept
We felt that the site would run best being "all flash". This would enable very fast access to our products, shopping cart and information. We found a way to code the site so that it would run like a html site. Back/fwd buttons, url changes and deeplinking to the product database. At the time of launch, we were the first site to do this.

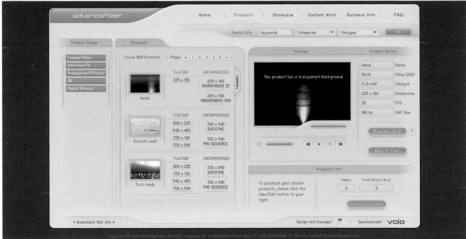

Info

DESIGN: Jay Birch <www.jaybirch.com>. /// **PROGRAMMING:** Void <www.void.pt>. /// **TOOLS:** Macromedia Flash, Adobe Photoshop, php, xml, MySql, JavaScript, ActionScript. /// **CONTENTS:** flash video and motion effects. /// **AWARDS:** FWA, TINY, American Website Awards, fcukstar. /// **COST:** 1000 hours.

Nous pensions que le site fonctionnerait mieux s'il était tout en Flash. Cela permet d'accéder à nos produits, au panier et aux informations très rapidement. Nous avons trouvé une façon de coder le site de sorte qu'il fonctionne comme un site HTML. Il y a des boutons avant/arrière, des changements d'URL et des liens profonds vers la base de données des produits. Au moment du lancement, nous étions le premier site à faire cela. /// Unserer Meinung nach sollte die gesamte Seite auf Flash basieren; dies würde einen schnellen Zugang zu all unseren Produkten, dem Einkaufswagen und Informationen gewährleisten. Wir haben eine Möglichkeit gefunden, die Seite so zu programmieren, dass sie wie eine HTML-Seite laufen würde: mit Vorwärts-/Rückwärts-Knöpfen, URL-Änderungen und Links zur Produktdatenbank. Zum Zeitpunkt der Einführung waren wir die erste Seite, auf der dies möglich war.

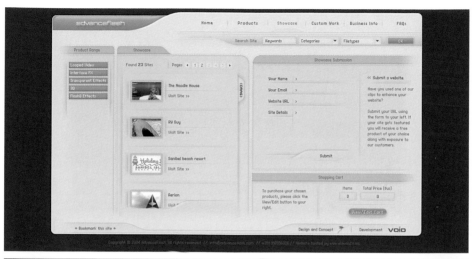

Concept

The brand Antonio Bernardo, in partnership with Americanas.com, one of the best-known e-commerce company in Latin America, has developed a new version for the previous institutional website. It was intended to ensure for its clients safety and quality in the eletronic commerce. Moreover, instead of becoming just a part of a multi-brand site, Antonio Bernardo Jewellery's identity was mantained on its own website, a pioneer initiative in the brazilian jewellery segment.

Info

DESIGN: Mariana Hermeto <www.marianahermeto.com.br>. /// PROGRAMMING: Americanas.com <www.americanas.com.br>. /// TOOLS: Adobe Photoshop, Macromedia Flash, ASP, Asp Net, SQL Server. /// CONTENTS: photo and animation. /// COST: 240 hours.

La marque Antonio Bernardo, en partenariat avec Americanas.com, l'une des entreprises d'e-commerce les plus connues d'Amérique latine, a développé une nouvelle version de l'ancien site institutionnel. Le but était de garantir à ses clients un commerce électronique sûr et de qualité. De plus, au lieu de n'être qu'une partie d'un site multimarques, la marque du joaillier Antonio Bernardo possède son propre site, une initiative pionnière dans le secteur de la joaillerie brésilienne. /// Die Marke Antonio Bernardo, in Partnerschaft mit Americanas.com, eines der bekanntesten E-Commerce-Unternehmen in Lateinamerika, hat eine neue Version der ehemaligen Webseite entwickelt, um ihren Kunden Sicherheit und Qualität im elektronischen Handel zu bieten. Anstatt nur Teil einer Seite mit mehreren Marken zu werden, wurde Antonio Bernardos Corporate Identity auf einer eigenen Webseite beibehalten – eine bahnbrechende Initiative im brasilianischen Schmucksegment.

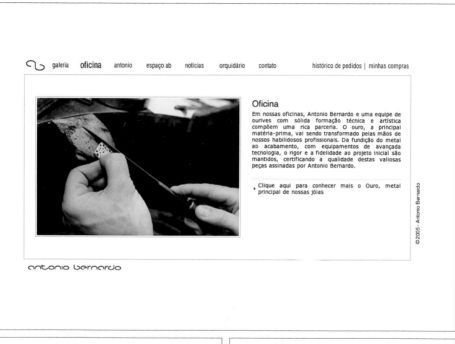

Concept

The site is about complete online fleetmanagement. The content of the website is presented in form of photos, flash animations, and rarely games.

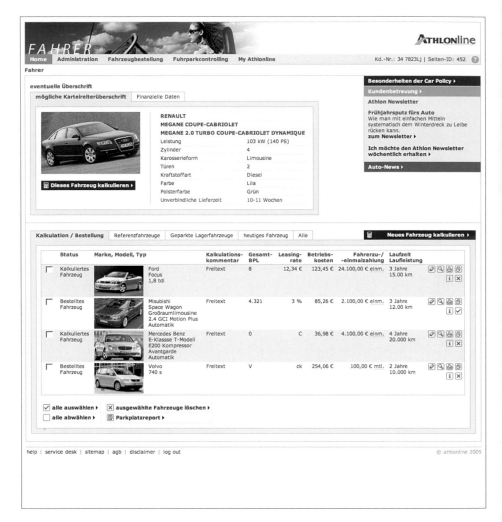

Info

DESIGN: wysiwyg* software design <www.wysiwyg.de>. /// PROGRAMMING: wysiwyg* and Athlon Car Lease <www.athloncarlease.de>. /// TOOLS: Html 4.01, CMS, php5, Adobe Photoshop, Adobe Illustrator, Macromedia Homesite, Adobe GoLIVE, CSS, JavaScript, MySql, Eclipse, Topstyle, Baldriparan. /// CONTENTS: photos, flash animations, rarely games. /// AWARDS: Autobranche Internet Award. /// COST: 2.800 hours.

Le site permet une gestion en ligne totale de la flotte de véhicules. Les contenus du site sont présentés sous forme de photos, d'animations Flash, et parfois de jeux. /// Diese Webseite präsentiert ein komplettes "Fleetmanagement" online. Der Inhalt wird in Form von Fotos, Flash-Animationen und einigen Spielen präsentiert.

Gehaltsumwandler

Athlon lease2motivate

ATHLON CAR LEASE

Gehaltsumwandler

Mit unserem Gehaltsumrechnungsmodell können Sie ganz einfach Schritt für Schritt Ihre persönlichen Kalkulationen durchführen. Verglichen wird dabei zwischen der Höhe des Nettogehaltsverzichts bei Gehaltsumwandlung und den Gesamtkosten für ein Privatauto auf Basis der ADAC-Fahrzeugvollkosten exkl. Kraftstoffkosten. Im ersten Schritt stellen wir Ihnen eine Auswahl der am meisten als Firmenwagen genutzten Leasingfahrzeuge dar. Um andere Fahrzeuge mit verschiedenen Ausstattungsmöglichkeiten zu kalkulieren, benutzen Sie bitte unsere Internetplattform

Kontakt ›
Quicktour ›
Wunschfahrzeug ›

Schritt 1 | Schritt 2 | Schritt 3 | Schritt 4 | Arbeitgeberkalkulation

Audi A3 Sportback MK2 2.0 TDI (DPF) Attraction

Bruttolistenpreis ir	In diesem Feld sehen Sie den Bruttolistenpreis Ihres
Laufleistung in km	Leasingfahrzeuges inkl. der
Leasinglaufzeit in	Ausstattung und Zubehör
Leasingrate in €	354,18 [i]
Kraftstoffkosten in €	92,40 [i]
Versicherung	ohne Versicherung [i]
Zubehör	nein [i]

Weiter mit Schritt 2 ›

ATLANTIC RECORDS

www.atlanticrecords.com

Concept

Atlanticrecords.com sought to become the first-ever major corporate label site to be considered a legitimate online resource by a Napster-friendly generation. Micro sites featured Atlantic Artists pages with music and video available for streaming, news, ring tones, lyrics, discussion boards, and CDs to order. A strong, stylish identity positioned Atlantic as powerful and modern while allowing the individual artists to shine.

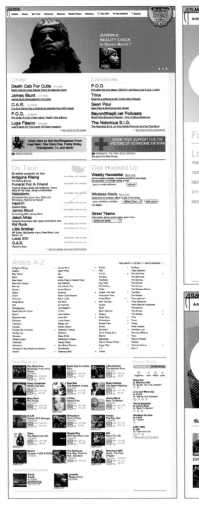

Info

DESIGN AND PROGRAMMING: HUGE <www.hugeinc.com>. /// TOOLS: Adobe Photoshop, Adobe Illustrator. /// CONTENTS: photos, illustrations, flash. /// COST: 9 months.

Atlanticrecords.com voulait devenir le premier site d'un grand label à être considéré comme une ressource en ligne légitime par la génération des enthousiastes de Napster. Des micro-sites présentent les pages des artistes d'Atlantic et diffusent de la musique et des vidéos, proposent des informations, des sonneries de portables, des paroles de chansons, des forums, et des CD à acheter. Une identité forte et élégante a donné à Atlantic l'image d'une entreprise moderne et puissante, tout en permettant à chaque artiste de briller de sa propre lumière. /// Atlanticrecords.com strebte danach, die erste große Unternehmensmarkenseite zu werden, die eine legale Online-Quelle für eine Napster-freundliche Generation darstellte. Mikroseiten enthielten Webseiten von Atlantic-Künstlern mit Musik, kleinen Filmen, Nachrichten, Klingeltönen, Songtexten, Diskussionsforen und der Möglichkeit, CDs zu bestellen. Ein starkes, schickes Image positionierte Atlantic als leistungsstark und modern und gab gleichzeitig den verschiedenen Künstlern die Möglichkeit, sich zu präsentieren.

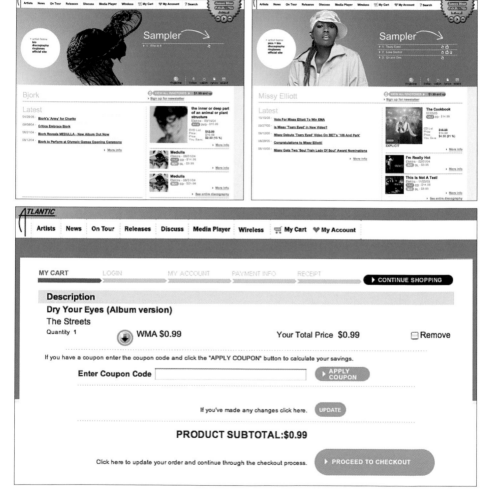

AXIO

www.axio-usa.com

USA

2005

Concept

The design of the Axio site is simple and minimalist, because of the unique nature of the packs we took the approach of less is more and made the product hero. Each pack or case can be viewed from multiple angles (open/ closed, side, back, front), several different colors options, close-up details pictures and various materials available to the customer.

Info DESIGN: Bob Haro (Creative Director Haro Design), Myles McGuinness (Creative Director/Designer): 9Myles <www.9myles.com>. /// PROGRAMMING: Ian Eyre <www.seventhform.com>. /// TOOLS: Macromedia Freehand, Adobe Illustrator, Macromedia Flash, Adobe Photoshop. /// CONTENTS: hard-shell and soft backpacks, ipod cases, plus accessories.

Le concept du site Axio est simple et minimaliste. C'est l'originalité des sacs qui nous a orienté vers cette approche, et nous avons donné la vedette au produit. On peut voir chaque sac ou pochette sous différents angles (ouvert/fermé, de côté, de face et de dos), ainsi que des gros plans de détails et les différentes options de couleur et de matières disponibles. /// Das Design der Axio-Seite ist einfach und minimalistisch, da wir im Zuge der Einzigartigkeit der Pakete vom Prinzip "Weniger ist mehr" ausgingen. Alle Pakete und Kisten können auf verschiedene Weise betrachtet werden (offen/geschlossen, von der Seite, von hinten, von vorn), und der Kunde kann zwischen unterschiedlichen Farben, Detailaufnahmen und Materialien wählen.

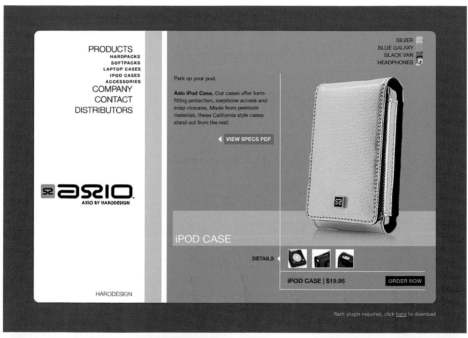

Concept

The real value of this e-commerce website is the mixing of different programming systems. The base made in flash cooperates efficiently with the asp part bothly technologically and graphically.

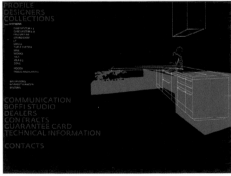

Info

DESIGN: Studio FM Milano <www.studiofmmilano.it>. /// **PROGRAMMING:** Park Media. /// **CONTENTS:** photos, animations, texts.

La véritable valeur de ce site d'e-commerce réside dans le mélange de différents systèmes de programmation. La base en Flash fonctionne efficacement avec la partie en ASP, à la fois du point de vue technologique et graphique. /// Der eigentliche Wert dieser E-Commerce-Webseite liegt in der Verwendung unterschiedlicher Programmiersysteme. Die Flash-Grundlage wirkt sowohl technisch als auch grafisch effizient mit dem ASP-Teil zusammen.

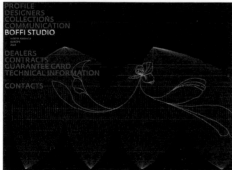

LE BUREAU DE TABAS

www.bureaudetabas.com

Concept

"Tabas' smoke shop" is made of various and divers' products, inspired by everyday life and all the little things surrounding me. One can find limited editions, hand-made odd craft, clothes, drawings, pictures, and even paintings. Some see signs, other see forms and contemporary patterns. I, on the other hand, try to input what I love and prefer and blend it all...

Info

DESIGN: Tabas <www.tabas.fr>. /// PROGRAMMING: KM817 <www.KM817.com>. /// TOOLS: html, php, JavaScript, MySql. /// CONTENTS: photos.

Le « bureau de Tabas » propose des produits divers et variés, inspirés de la vie quotidienne et de toutes les petites choses qui m'entourent. On y trouve des éditions limitées, des objets bizarres, des vêtements, des dessins, des images, et même des tableaux. Certains voient des signes, d'autres voient des formes et des motifs contemporains. Moi, j'essaie d'y mettre ce que j'aime et que je préfère et de tout mélange. /// Im "Tabas' smoke shop" gibt es viele unterschiedliche Produkte, die vom alltäglichen Leben und den Dingen, die mich umgeben, inspiriert sind. Man findet Bücher mit begrenzten Auflagen, den ein oder anderen handgemachten Zierrat, Kleidung, Zeichnungen, Bilder und sogar Gemälde. Einige sehen in diesen Bildern Zeichen, andere Formen und zeitgenössische Muster. Ich selbst hingegen neige dazu, alles, was ich mag, hinein zu interpretieren und zu vermischen.

Concept

Clyde's Online is the online home of Clyde's on Madison, the upper east side's most upscale pharmacy. They offer fine European bath and body products, cosmetics, fragrances and more. Firstborn combined Commerce Server and Flash MX to create e-commerce with the Firstborn touch – an exciting, dynamic and stylish shopping experience.

Info

DESIGN AND PROGRAMMING: Firstborn <www.firstbornmultimedia.com>. /// TOOLS: Adobe Photoshop, Macromedia Flash MX, Macromedia Dreamweaver MX, Microsoft SQL Server, Microsoft Commerce Server, Microsoft ASP.NET, Authorize.net (payment gateway). /// CONTENTS: imagery, and product information. /// AWARDS: Macromedia Case Study. /// COST: 800 hours.

Clyde's Online est le site de Clyde de Madison Avenue, la pharmacie la plus chic de l'Upper East Side. Il propose des produits européens raffinés pour le bain et le soin du corps, des cosmétiques, des parfums et bien plus encore. Firstborn a combiné Commerce Server et Flash MX pour créer un e-commerce avec la griffe Firstborn : un site d'achat captivant, dynamique et élégant. /// Clyde's Online ist die Online-Plattform von Clyde's auf der Madison Avenue, die beste Drogerie der East Side. Sie bietet Körperpflegeprodukte aus Europa, Kosmetik, Düfte und mehr an. Firstborn kombinierte Commerce-Server und Flash MX, um E-Commerce mit dem Firstborn-Touch zu kreieren – ein faszinierendes, dynamisches und luxuriöses Einkaufserlebnis.

COFT1

www.coft1.com

GERMANY

2004

Concept

Coft1 tries to combine high quality Design Shirts with an aesthetic but at the same time easy to use Interface. It is at the same time the Online Shop of the studio stereoplastic.com.

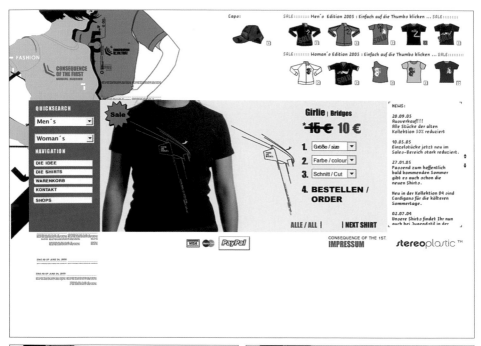

Info

DESIGN: Mike John Otto / stereoplastic.com <www.stereoplastic.com>. /// **PROGRAMMING:** Mike John Otto, Jan Riggert. /// **TOOLS:** Adobe Photoshop, Macromedia Flash, Macromedia Dreamweaver, Macromedia Freehand, php. /// **CONTENTS:** photo, animation. /// **AWARDS:** k10k, plasticpilots, BD4D. /// **COST:** 2 months.

Coft1 essaie de combiner des T-shirts de créateurs de grande qualité avec une interface esthétique, mais facile à utiliser. C'est aussi la boutique en ligne du studio stereoplastic.com. /// **Coft1 versucht, hochwertige ästhetische Designs mit einer einfachen Benutzeroberfläche zu kombinieren. Es ist gleichzeitig der Online-Shop des Studios stereoplastic.com.**

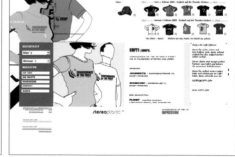

COLETTE PARIS

www.colette.fr

Concept

The most fun e-commerce site around!

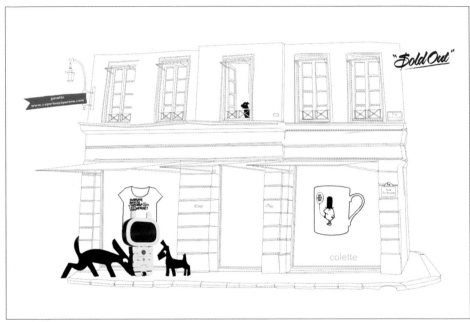

product

Irina by Fafi

× 90

send this to
a friend

buy this product

Irina by Fafi

French graffiti princess Fafi teams up with
the Necessaries Toy Foundation to produce
her first ever figurine "Irina" with a special
"purple jacket" edition just for colette.
And there's cap's too: with each design
individually customised by the artist herself.

height : 33 cm

www.fafi.net

Info

DESIGN AND PROGRAMMING: Spill.net <www.spill.net>. /// TOOLS: Macromedia Flash, xml, UI-Pro, php, mysql, Adobe Photoshop. /// CONTENTS: photos, music, films, animation, texts. /// AWARDS: Webby Award. /// COST: 240 hours.

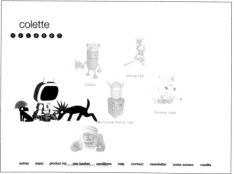

Concept

There are two basic differences between Estrela Guia e-commerce and conventional e-commerce. First, the site products are totally personalised (every map is unique, depending on such variables as place, time and date of birth), i.e., there are different products for each user. Secondly, the product is delivered in real time, via the Internet and e-mail. Delivery is Internet-based, 100% virtual, 100% digital.

Info

DESIGN: Estrela Guia <www.estrelaguia.com.br>. /// PROGRAMMING: Rodolfo Fiuza. /// TOOLS: Linux, FreeBsd, php, Perl, Apache. /// CONTENTS: Astrology, Horoscope, Tarot, etc. /// AWARDS: Ibest 2004, Ibest 2005.

Il y a deux grandes différences entre l'e-commerce d'Estrela Guía et l'e-commerce conventionnel. Tout d'abord, les produits du site sont totalement personnalisés (chaque carte est unique, en fonction de variables telles que le lieu, l'heure et la date de naissance), c'est-à-dire qu'à chaque utilisateur correspondent des produits différents. Ensuite, le produit est livré en temps réel, par Internet et par e-mail. La livraison se passe entièrement sur Internet, 100 % virtuelle, 100 % numérique. /// Es gibt zwei grundlegende Unterschiede zwischen Estrela Guía E-Commerce und herkömmlichem E-Commerce. Erstens sind die Produkte der Seite vollkommen individualisiert (jede Karte ist einzigartig, je nach Ort, Zeit und Geburtsdatum), d.h. für jeden Benutzer gibt es unterschiedliche Produkte. Zweitens wird das Produkt in Echtzeit über Internet und Email geliefert. Die Lieferung erfolgt über das Internet – 1005 virtuell, 100% digital.

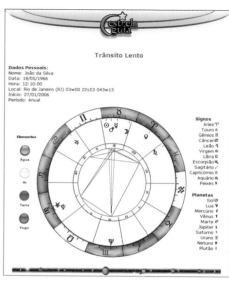

FCUK FRAGRANCE

www.fcukfragrance.com

Concept

Firstborn combines Flash and e-commerce for UK fashion retailer, French Connection. For the launch, licensee Zirh International developed this edgy, modern and sexy new fragrance for men and women, cleverly known as fcuk him and fcuk her.

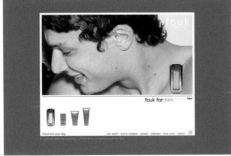

Info

DESIGN AND PROGRAMMING: Firstborn <www.firstbornmultimedia.com>. /// **TOOLS:** Adobe Photoshop CS, Macromedia Flash MX, Macromedia Dreamweaver MX, Microsoft SQL Server, Microsoft Commerce Server, Microsoft ASP.NET, XML, Authorize.net (payment gateway), TripleFin (fulfillment partner), WebTrends (tracking). /// **CONTENTS:** audio, imagery, and product information. /// **AWARDS:** Macromedia (Site of the Day). /// **COST:** 700 hours.

Firstborn combine Flash et e-commerce pour les boutiques de mode britanniques French Connection. Pour le lancement, le concessionnaire Zirh International a créé ce nouveau parfum énergique, actuel et sexy pour hommes et femmes, rebaptisé fcuk him et fcuk her par la rue. /// Firstborn kombiniert Flash und E-Commerce für den Modehändler French Connection aus Großbritannien. Für die Einführung entwickelte der Lizenzinhaber Zirh International einen modernen und sexy Duft für Männer und Frauen, bekannt als fcuk him und fcuk her.

FEEL THE POWER

www.feelthepower.biz

Concept

Most e-commerce sites are HTML catalogs. FeelThePower.biz is an immersive, motion graphics experience that creates a brand experience while selling product.

Info

DESIGN AND PROGRAMMING: Freedom Interactive <www.freedominteractivedesign.com>. /// TOOLS: MS SQL Server, Macromedia Flash, Adobe Photoshop. /// CONTENTS: sports performance apparel. /// AWARDS: FWA. /// COST: 550 hours.

La plupart des sites d'e-commerce sont des catalogues en HTML. FeelThePower.biz vous plonge dans des graphismes animés et crée une identité de marque tout en vendant un produit. /// Die meisten E-Commerce-Seiten sind HTML-Kataloge. FeelThePower.biz hingegen ist eine faszinierende Seite mit beweglichen Grafiken, die ein Markenerlebnis schafft und gleichzeitig Produkte verkauft.

FILATIVA

www.filativa.com

Concept

Firstborn steps it up for legendary shoe company, Fila, and their launch of the new Filativa line of fashionable kicks. Fila's fusion concept combines their Italian heritage with a New York vibe to create these comfortable and stylish shoes. Firstborn designed an engaging website to showcase the brand and make it easy to shop online. We partnered with many vendors to provide advanced functionality to the site, including Oracle, Akamai, Live Person, Where2Getit and others.

Info

DESIGN AND PROGRAMMING: Firstborn <www.firstbornmultimedia.com>. /// TOOLS: Adobe Photoshop CS, Macromedia Flash MX, Macromedia Dreamweaver MX. Partners: Oracle iStore, Oracle Database, Scene 7 (image zoom), Where2GetIt (retail locator), Coremetrics (tracking), Live Person (customer service). /// CONTENTS: audio, imagery, and product information. /// AWARDS: 2005 Webaward (Standard of Excellence). /// COST: 1.000 hours.

Firstborn s'est dépassé pour la légendaire marque de chaussures Fila avec le lancement de sa nouvelle ligne, Filativa. Fila fusionne ses racines italiennes avec l'atmosphère de New York pour créer ces chaussures confortables et élégantes. Firstborn a imaginé un site engageant pour présenter la marque et permettre aux clients d'acheter en ligne facilement. Nous avons travaillé en collaboration avec de nombreux fournisseurs pour doter le site de fonctionnalités avancées, dont Oracle, Akamai, Live Person et Where2Getit, entre autres. /// Firstborn schaltet für das legendäre Schuhunternehmen Fila und die Einführung ihrer neuen Filativa-Linie modischer KICKS noch eine Stufe höher. Filas Fusionskonzept kombiniert bei der Entwicklung dieser schicken, bequemen Schuhe ihre italienische Herkunft mit einem New York-Vibe. Firstborn gestaltete eine einnehmende Webseite, um die Marke darzustellen und den Einkauf online zu erleichtern. Wir arbeiteten mit vielen Verkäufern zusammen, um eine fortschrittliche Funktionalität der Seite zu bieten, darunter Oracle, Akamai, Live Person, Where2Getit und andere.

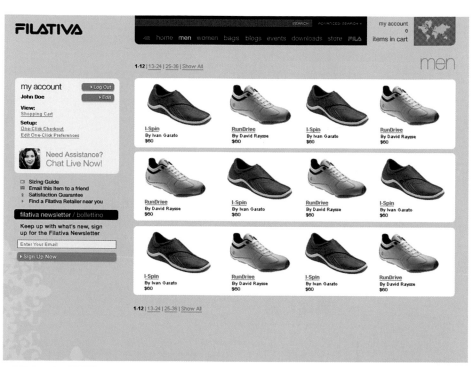

FORD VEHICLES

www.fordvehicles.com

Concept

Fordvehicles.com was built to be a completely dynamic Flash system, generating a Rich Media interface through XML feeds and to be fully manageable by the client. Presenting Ford with a powerful web presence, clean design and concise navigation gave them a superior market position over their competitors and made it very easy for them to satisfy the Ford customers.

Info

DESIGN AND PROGRAMMING: Fantasy Interactive <www.fantasy-interactive.com>. /// TOOLS: In the development we used, among others, ActionScript 2.0, JavaScript, Visual Studio.Net, PrimalScript and for file management we used SourceSafe. Adobe Photoshop and Macromedia Flash were our primary tools in creating the design and interactivity. /// CONTENTS: interactive presentation of all Ford Division cars, SUVs, minivans and trucks. /// AWARDS: FWA (Site of the Day). /// COST: 1 month.

Fordvehicles.com est un système Flash totalement dynamique qui génère une interface Rich Media alimentée en XML. Le client peut gérer tout le site. Cette présence Internet solide, au style élégant et à la navigation limpide a donné à Ford de l'avance sur ses concurrents et est un instrument incomparable pour la satisfaction de ses clients. /// Fordvehicles.com sollte ein komplett dynamisches Flash-System werden, indem man eine Rich-Media-Oberfläche mit XML generierte, die vom Kunden verwendet werden konnte. Durch diesen starken Webauftritt mit klarem Design und präziser Navigation verschaffte man Ford eine stärkere Marktposition gegenüber der Konkurrenz und verhalf ihnen dazu, ihre Kunden zufrieden zu stellen.

FREDDY & MA

USA

2006

www.freddyandma.com

Concept: Freddy & Ma's customers can design and order their own custom handbags. Domani' Studios' custom-built configurator weds dynamic data with interactive Flash to put everything at your virtual fingertips: bag styles, leather colors, and hundreds of prints. Each step of the way, the bag takes shape right before your eyes. On checkout, an order is placed at the factory for your unique creation.

Info: **DESIGN AND PROGRAMMING:** Domani Studios <www.domanistudios.com>. /// **TOOLS:** Flash, XML, PHP, MySQL, Proprietary store CMS. ///
CONTENTS: Custom-built animated handbag configuration tool, photos, animations. /// **COST:** 500 hours.

Les clients de Freddy & Ma peuvent créer et commander leurs propres sacs personnalisés. Le module de configuration réalisé sur mesure par Domani' Studios combine données dynamiques et interactivité en Flash pour vous donner les moyens virtuels d'exprimer votre créativité : jouez avec les styles de sacs, les couleurs de cuir, et des centaines de motifs. À chaque étape, le sac prend forme sous vos yeux. Puis l'usine reçoit la commande de votre création originale.

/// Die Kunden von Freddy & Ma können hier ihre eigenen Handtaschen entwerfen und bestellen. Domani Studios speziell angefertigter Konfigurator vereinigt dynamische Daten mit interaktivem Flash, sodass alles virtuell zur Verfügung steht: verschiedene Stile, Lederfarben und Hunderte von Mustern. Mit jedem Schritt nimmt die Tasche auf dem Bildschirm Form an. Mit dem Checkout erfolgt eine Bestellung in der Fabrik für Ihren individuellen Entwurf.

FRED PERRY

www.fredperry.com

Concept

The site blends elegance and simplicity to offer a stylish and intuitive way to purchase garments. Understated, but with high levels of attention to detail – reflecting Fred Perry brand values. The unique heritage of the brand is given contemporary relevance by the Subculture music section. Listen to cutting edge music, whilst viewing cutting edge British street style. Users love it.

enter fredperry.com

Info

DESIGN AND PROGRAMMING: De Facto Design <www.de-facto.com>. /// **TOOLS:** HTML, Microsoft ASP, Macromedia Flash, Macromedia Freehand, Adobe Photoshop, Bare Bones BBEdit. /// **CONTENTS:** clothing, photography, music. /// **AWARDS:** FWA (Site of the Day). /// **COST:** 720 hours.

Le site marie raffinement et simplicité pour présenter à ses clients une manière élégante et intuitive d'acheter des vêtements. Discret mais sophistiqué, il reflète les valeurs de la marque Fred Perry. L'héritage unique de la marque est actualisé par la partie « Subculture music » du site. Les utilisateurs adorent écouter cette musique d'avant-garde tout en parcourant ses vêtements britanniques à la pointe de la mode urbaine. /// Diese Seite kombiniert Eleganz und Einfachheit und bietet so einen stilvollen und leicht verständlichen Weg, Kleidung zu kaufen. Unaufdringlich, aber mit viel Rücksicht auf Details, reflektiert die Seite die Eigenschaften der Marke Fred Perry. Die einzigartige Herkunft der Marke erhält durch die unterlegte alternative Musik zeitgenössische Relevanz. Aktuelle Musik hören, während man den neuesten britischen Straßenschick betrachtet – die Benutzer lieben es.

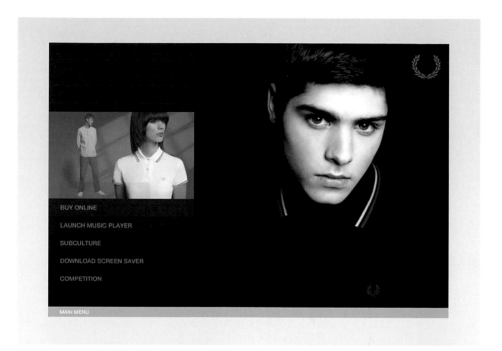

FUN FACTORY

www.funfactory.de

GERMANY

2006

Concept

A simple and objective solution to sell a niche product worldwide. Very direct and easy-to-use approach.

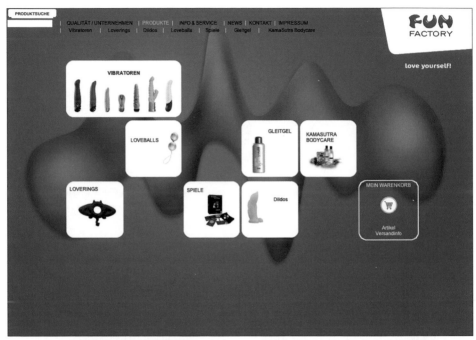

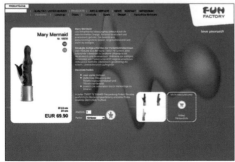

Info

DESIGN: höwel werbung — gd <www.hwgd.de>. /// **TOOLS:** html, css, php, Adobe Photoshop, Adobe InDesign, MySQL. /// **CONTENTS:** shop, news, photo gallery, spots, customer-, retailer & press-information.

Une solution simple et objective pour vendre dans le monde entier un produit destiné à un marché de niche. Une approche très directe et conviviale. /// Eine einfache und sachliche Möglichkeit, ein Nischenprodukt weltweit zu vertreiben. Sehr direkt und einfach zu verwenden.

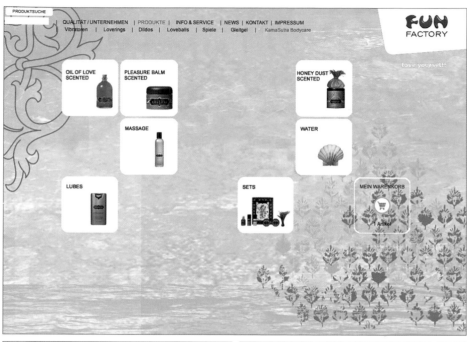

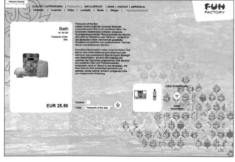

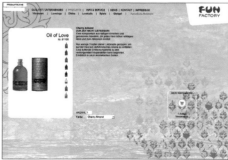

GEORGINA GOODMAN

www.georginagoodman.com/shop

Concept

Luxury is hard to sell, but with DS9 providing the design output, it can be bought.

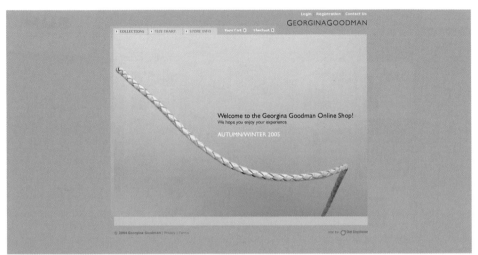

Info

DESIGN: Diet Strychnine Corp. <www.dietstrychnine.com>. /// **PROGRAMMING:** Chris Daou & Rick Gutierrez (Diet Strychnine Corp.). /// **TOOLS:** Adobe Photoshop, Adobe Illustrator, Macromedia Dreamweaver, php, dhtml. /// **CONTENTS:** photo. /// **AWARDS:** Communication Arts Interactive. /// **COST:** 300 hours.

Pas facile de vendre du luxe, mais avec D59 aux commandes du site, cela s'achète très bien. /// Luxus lässt sich nur schwer verkaufen, aber mit der Design-leistung von D59 lässt er sich kaufen.

GERMANWINGS

www.germanwings.com

Concept

The Germanwings site is a 'smart travel portal' providing state-of-the-art functionality. The site is localized for 20 countries and available in 20 languages. Customers can manage their bookings online using the 'My Germanwings' area of the site and book services from partners who are directly interfaced with the site. The site is structured to meet the specific needs of three target groups: 'speed bookers', 'idea browsers' and bargain hunters.

Info

DESIGN: Neue Digitale <www.neue-digitale.de>. /// PROGRAMMING: Web-Development Germanwings and IT Eurowings. /// AWARDS: Focus-Test, FVW International, Eurobest Award (Silber); New York Festivals Interactive (Bronze); CRESTA 2005 (Winner); ADC New York (Silber); The One Show Interactive 2005 (Silber); ADC Deutschland 2005 (Silber).

Le site de Germanwings est un « portail de voyage intelligent » qui propose des fonctionnalités dernier cri. Le site est décliné pour 20 pays et est disponible en 20 langues. Les clients peuvent gérer leurs réservations en ligne en utilisant la partie « My Germanwings » du site et réserver des services auprès de partenaires qui possèdent une interface directe avec le site. La structure du site a pour mission de satisfaire les besoins spécifiques de trois groupes cibles : les « voyageurs pressés », les « chercheurs d'idée », et les « chasseurs de bonnes affaires ». /// Die Germanwings-Seite ist ein "cleveres Reiseportal", das Funktionalität auf dem neuesten Stand der Technik bietet. Die Seite ist für 20 Länder angelegt und in 20 Sprachen verfügbar. Kunden können im "My Germanwings"-Bereich nicht nur Flüge online buchen, sondern auch Serviceleistungen von Partnern, die direkt mit der Seite verlinkt sind. Die Seite ist so aufgebaut, dass sie den speziellen Bedürfnissen von drei Zielgruppen entspricht: "Schnellbucher", "Ideensucher" und Schnäppchenjäger.

Concept

A great example of how niche sites can be special and can offer direct solutions to users. The concept has been originated in a book series, showing as well how media today can interact between digital and printed.

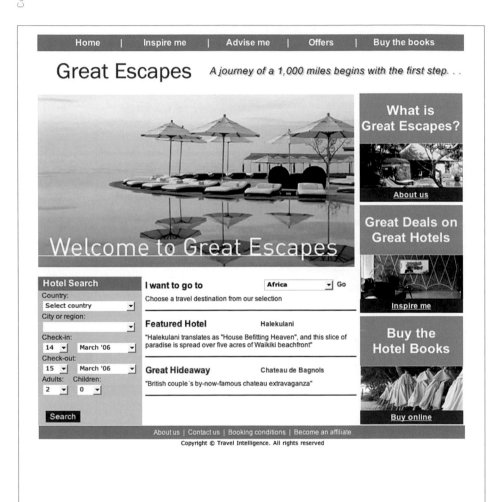

Info

DESIGN: Travel Intelligence <www.travelintelligence.com>. /// PROGRAMMING: Mango Software <www.mangosoftware.nl>. /// TOOLS: XML, Xhtml. ///
CONTENTS: photos, multi lingual descriptions of hotels, online hotel reservation functionality, catered to Taschen's Hotel Book series. ///
COST: 253 hours.

Un excellent exemple de site spécialisé qui a su se rendre original et offrir des solutions directes à ses utilisateurs. Le concept est né d'une série de livres, ce qui montre bien que les médias actuels peuvent combiner le numérique et l'imprimé. /// Ein gutes Bespiel dafür, wie Nischenseiten etwas ganz Besonderes sein können und Benutzern einfache Lösungen anbieten. Das Konzept war ursprünglich eine Buchreihe – dies zeigt, wie digitale und Printmedien heutzutage interagieren.

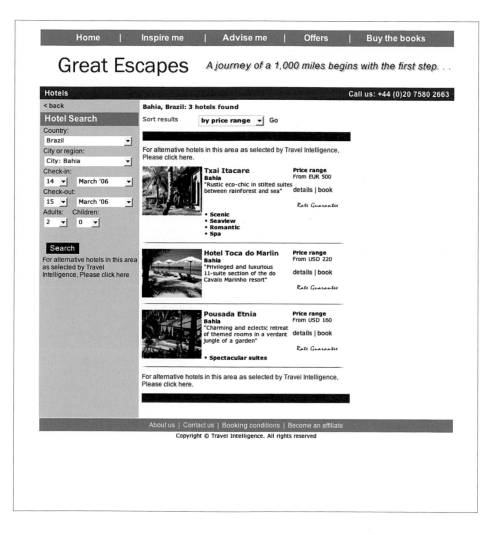

HEFTY RECORDS

USA

www.heftyrecords.com

2006

Concept

HEFTY! Records distinguishes itself by operating as a hybrid between an informational site and an e-commerce site. The storefront is woven with data about artists, albums, tours and the label and is linked to an online radio. A halo of record albums surrounds the site, moving in and out as you browse information and products - graphically bridging the store areas with the remainder of the site.

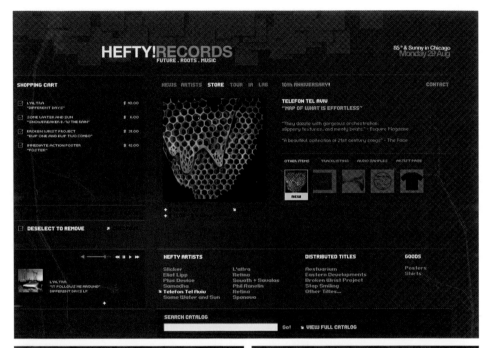

Info

DESIGN AND PROGRAMMING: TENDER CREATIVE <www.tendercreative.com>. /// TOOLS: PHP, xml, Macromedia Flash, Adobe Photoshop, MySql. /// CONTENTS: music, photo, video.

HEFTY ! Records est un site hybride, il combine information et e-commerce. La boutique fourmille de données sur les artistes, les albums et les concerts, et le label est relié à une radio en ligne. Une couronne d'albums entoure le site, et ses éléments vont et viennent sur la page au gré de votre navigation dans les informations et les produits, et créent un pont entre les différentes zones du site. /// HEFTY! Records unterscheidet sich von anderen Seiten durch seine Mischung zwischen einer Informations- und E-Commerce-Seite. Die Fassade enthält Informationen über Künstler, Alben, Tourneen und das Label und ist mit einem Online-Radio verlinkt. Die Seite wird von Plattenalben eingerahmt, die sich auf dem Bildschirm bewegen, während man sich nach Informationen und Produkten umsieht. Dadurch ist der Kaufbereich grafisch mit dem Rest der Seite verknüpft.

IPPOLITA

http://ippolita.com

Concept

Ippolita.com breaks from the dull, predictable "catalog model" for page layout and site architecture that's too common in ecommerce sites. The clean and modern page layout emphasizes the product imagery—beautiful artistic photos that evoke the romance of fine jewelry. An unobtrusive Flash shopping cart expands at the shopper's request, never taking her away from Ippolita's beautifully-crafted treasures.

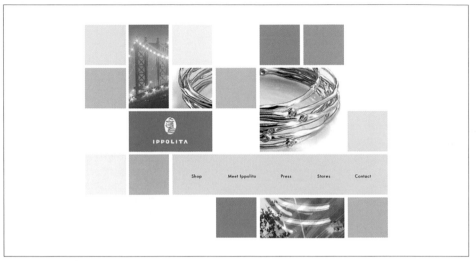

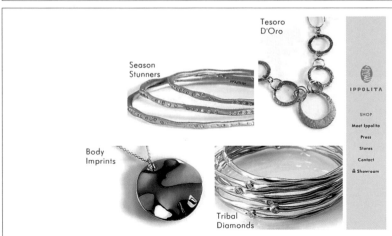

Info

DESIGN AND PROGRAMMING: Domani Studios <domanistudios.com>. /// **TOOLS:** Macromedia Flash, MySQL, PHP, Proprietary store CMS. /// **CONTENTS:** digital photography, flash shopping cart. /// **COST:** 300 hours.

Ippolita.com rompt avec les modèles de catalogues ternes et prévisibles dont la mise en page et l'architecture sont trop courantes dans les sites d'e-commerce. Ici, la mise en page élégante et moderne met en valeur la présentation des produits. Les magnifiques photos artistiques font écho au charme des bijoux précieux. Le panier d'achats en Flash, discret, se développe à la demande du client mais ne lui cache jamais les trésors artistiques d'Ippolita. /// Ippolita.com bricht mit dem langweiligen, vorhersehbaren "Katalogmodell" des bei E-Commerce-Seiten üblichen Layouts und Seitenaufbaus. Das klare und moderne Seitenlayout betont das Produktimage: Schöne, künstlerische Fotos beschwören die Romantik edler Schmuckstücke herauf. Ein unauffälliger Einkaufswagen erweitert sich durch Flash, wie es der Einkauf erfordert, und lenkt die Aufmerksamkeit nie von Ippolitas schönem Schmuck ab.

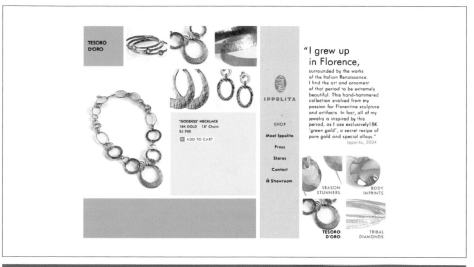

YOUR JEWELRY CART: 1 item   close cart ☒

"Goddess" Necklace
GN007

Option Selected: N/A
Unit Price: 3,900.00
Sub Total: 3,900.00

▶ QUANTITY: 1

Your Current Order:

Order Sub Total: $3,900.00
Shipping and Handling: $18.00
_____
ESTIMATED TOTAL: **$3,918.00**

International orders please call
1-877-865-5500

▶ CHECKOUT

▶ CONTINUE SHOPPING

Concept

Going beyond a one-dimensional call/response airline e-commerce model, the JetBlue Getaways site aims to inspire its pages' visitors as they consider vacation options. In addition to providing the tools to conveniently book trip airfare and accommodations at a single site, Getaways is an abbreviated guidebook meant to excite travelers about their possible destinations and allow them to build their own vacation packages.

Info

DESIGN AND PROGRAMMING: HUGE <www.hugeinc.com>. /// TOOLS: Adobe Photoshop, Adobe Illustrator. /// CONTENTS: photos, illustrations, copywriting. /// COST: 3 months.

Au-delà du modèle unidimensionnel appel/réponse des lignes aériennes sur Internet, le site jetBlue Getaways souhaite inspirer ses visiteurs en quête d'idées de vacances. Getaways fournit à ses clients les outils pour réserver commodément leurs billets d'avion et leur logement sur un même site, mais c'est aussi un petit guide qui piquera la curiosité des voyageurs et leur permettra d'organiser leurs vacances. /// Diese Seite übersteigt das eindimensionale Anfrage/Antwort-Modell von E-Commerce Fluganbietern und will so die Benutzer, die nach Urlaubsmöglichkeiten suchen, inspirieren. Es werden nicht nur Methoden zur bequemen Buchung von Flügen und Unterkünften auf einer einzelnen Seite bereitgestellt, sondern auch ein verkürzter Ratgeber, der den Reisenden über die möglichen Reiseziele informiert und die Zusammenstellung individueller Urlaubspauschalreisen ermöglicht.

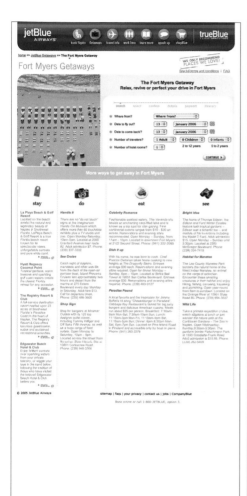

Concept

We combined style and shopping for fashion designer John Varvatos as he launched his first fragrance collection. We've integrated Flash and eCommerce to create a unique experience for the elegant, masculine and sensual new scent developed by licensee Zirh International.

Info

DESIGN AND PROGRAMMING: Firstborn <www.firstbornmultimedia.com>. /// TOOLS: Adobe Photoshop CS, Macromedia Flash MX, Macromedia Dreamweaver MX, Microsoft SQL Server, Microsoft Commerce Server, Microsoft ASP.NET, XML, Authorize.net (payment gateway), TripleFin (fulfillment partner), WebTrends (tracking). /// CONTENTS: audio, imagery, and product information. /// AWARDS: FWA (Winner). /// COST: 700 hours.

Nous avons combiné style et shopping pour le lancement de la première collection de parfums du créateur de mode John Varvatos. Nous avons intégré Flash et e-commerce afin de créer un site original pour le nouveau parfum élégant, masculin et sensuel créé par le concessionnaire Zirh International. /// Wir kombinierten Eleganz und Einkauf für den Modedesigner John Varvatos, als er seine erste Duftkollektion einführte. Durch die Integration von Flash und E-Commerce schufen wir ein einzigartiges Einkaufserlebnis für den eleganten, männlichen und sinnlichen Duft, der vom Lizenzinhaber Zirh International entwickelt worden war.

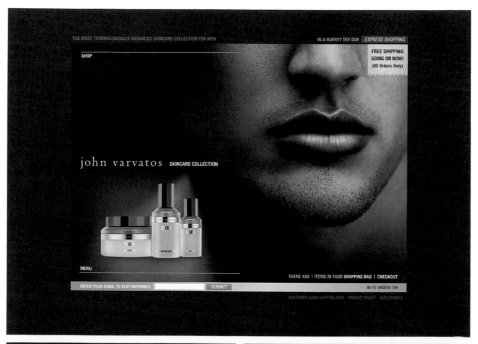

Concept

As it is said: Landlords come and go, but the guests stay. For breweries within a highly competitive market it becomes more and more important to work out their claims in the catering trade segment. The Krombacher brand presents the user a detailed survey of the vacancies and information about every single object for every location in order to enable talented gastronomes to find their regulars.

Info

DESIGN AND PROGRAMMING: wysiwyg* software design <www.wysiwyg.de>. /// TOOLS: Html 4.01, CMS, php, Adobe Photoshop, Adobe GoLIVE, CSS, JavaScript, MySql, Eclipse. /// CONTENTS: photos, descriptions.

L'adage populaire dit que les patrons ne font que passer, seuls les clients restent fidèles ! Sur le marché très concurrentiel de la bière, les brasseries ont tout intérêt à marquer leur présence dans le segment de la gastronomie. C'est ce que la marque Krombacher fait activement : Krombacher publie sur son site une liste détaillée des établissements vacants, ainsi que des informations sur chacun d'entre eux et sur sa situation, afin que des restaurateurs talentueux trouvent la clientèle fidèle qu'ils méritent. /// Der Volksmund sagt, dass Wirte kommen und gehen – aber die Gäste immer bleiben. Und für Brauereien wird es in einem hart umkämpften Biermarkt wichtiger, ihre Claims auch in dem Segment der Gastronomie abzustecken. Die Marke Krombacher bietet deshalb auf ihrer Website eine umfangreiche Übersicht der Vakanzen und Detailinformationen zu jedem einzelnen interessanten Objekt und zu jeder Location – damit talentierte Gastronomen noch besser zu ihrem Stammpublikum finden können.

KROMBACHER ONLINE SHOP

www.krombacher.de/shop

Concept

The online shop of the Krombacher brand has a distinctive advantage: It is simple. Therefore, the relaunch has paid for itself already after 3 months. There are no license costs or fees for the shop system because the entire technique is based on Open Source.

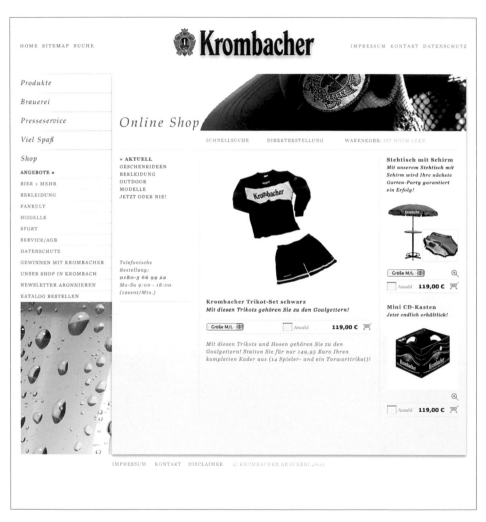

Info

DESIGN AND PROGRAMMING: wysiwyg* software design <www.wysiwyg.de>. /// TOOLS: Html 4.01, CMS, php, Adobe Photoshop, Adobe Illustrator, Macromedia Homesite, Adobe GoLIVE, CSS, JavaScript, MySql, Eclipsel. /// CONTENTS: photos, descriptions.

La boutique en ligne de la marque Krombacher présente un immense avantage : elle est facile à utiliser. Après trois mois à peine, l'investissement dans la refonte du site est déjà amorti. Aucuns frais de licence pour la boutique en ligne, car la conception est entièrement basée sur les techniques « open source ».
/// Der Online-Shop der Marke Krombacher hat einen entscheidenden Vorteil: Er ist einfach. Deswegen hat sich die Investition in den Relaunch bereits nach 3 Monaten amortisiert. Lizenzkosten oder Gebühren für das Shopsystem fallen nicht an, da die gesamte Technik auf Open Source basiert.

LAVETT & CHIN

http://lavettandchin.com

Concept Sexy and glamorous... ecommerce? This website is a marketing and branding tool, not just a store. By integrating video from a model shoot seamlessly into a Flash interface, we literally show the world that Lavett & Chin means beauty and sophistication. Furthermore, the overlying Flash shopping cart and subtle animations feel as organic and natural as Lavett & Chin's products.

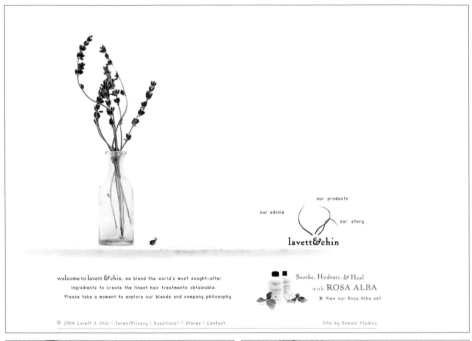

Info DESIGN AND PROGRAMMING: Domani Studios <www.domanistudios.com>. /// TOOLS: Macromedia Flash, digital video, MySQL, PHP, Proprietary store CMS. /// CONTENTS: Flash with integrated digital video, flash. /// AWARDS: Communication Arts: Interactive (Best Sites of the Year); STEP Magazine: best of the web (top 50 must-see websites). /// COST: 400 hours.

Sexy, glamour et... e-commerce ? Ce site est un instrument de marketing et de promotion de marque, pas seulement une boutique. En intégrant la vidéo d'une session de photos dans une interface Flash, nous montrons littéralement au monde que Lavett & Chin est synonyme de beauté et de sophistication. De plus, le panier d'achats en superposition et les animations subtiles sont aussi naturels et organiques que les produits de Lavett & Chin. /// E-Commerce – sexy und glamourös? Diese Webseite ist nicht nur ein Shop, sondern auch ein Marketing- und Markeninstrument. Indem wir das Video einer Modellaufnahme nahtlos mit einer Flash-Oberfläche kombinierten, konnten wir der Welt buchstäblich zeigen, dass Lavett & Chin Schönheit und Kultiviertheit bedeutet. Zusätzlich muten die darüber liegenden Flash-Einkaufswagen und raffinierten Animationen genauso organisch und natürlich an wie die Produkte.

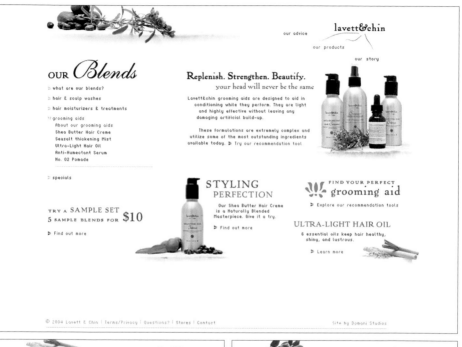

Concept
The LogoYes website features a patent-pending Flash-based application which enables small business owners to create customized logos online in minutes. Customers do not need any experience in graphic design – they simply choose a symbol (from a database of 20,000 images), select a font, modify colors, and rotate or resize until satisfied with their logo. In addition, the "try-before-you-buy" process ensures customer satisfaction.

Info
DESIGN: John Williams (LogoYes). /// PROGRAMMING: Brad Jackson and Rob Skelly (2 Advanced Studios). /// TOOLS: Macromedia Flash, PHP, C, FreeType, ImageMagick, and various other command-line based utilities. /// CONTENTS: application. /// AWARDS: WMA Web Award's Outstanding Website Award, FWA (Site of the Day), Flash Kit's (Winning Site Award). /// COST: 6 months.

L'application Flash du site LogoYes, en cours d'obtention de brevet, propose aux chefs de petites entreprises de créer en ligne des logos personnalisés en quelques minutes. Les clients n'ont besoin d'aucune expérience en graphisme : ils choisissent simplement un symbole (dans une base de données de 20 000 images), sélectionnent une police de caractères, puis modifient les couleurs et ajustent l'orientation ou la taille de leur logo jusqu'à ce qu'ils soient satisfaits. De plus, le procédé « essayez avant d'acheter » est une garantie de satisfaction. /// Die LogoYes-Webseite enthält eine noch nicht patentierte Flash-basierte Anwendung, mit der Eigentümer von Kleinunternehmen innerhalb von Minuten Logos nach ihrem eigenen Wunsch online entwerfen können. Hierfür benötigen die Kunden keine Erfahrung im Grafikdesign – sie wählen einfach ein Symbol (aus einer Datenbank mit 20 000 Bildern) und eine Schriftart aus, verändern die Farben und drehen und vergrößern oder verkleinern ihr Logo so lange, bis sie zufrieden sind. Der "try-before-you-buy"-Prozess gewährleistet die Zufriedenheit des Kunden.

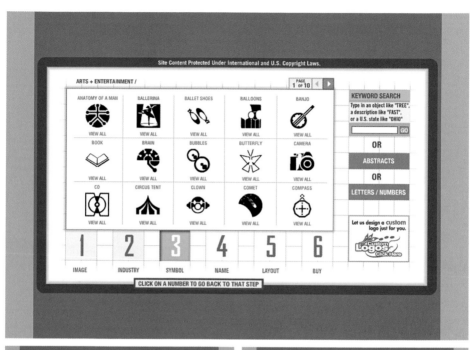

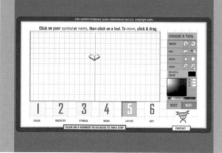

BLINDE: MATRIX COLLECTION USA

http://staging.glowinteractive.com/matrix   2003

Concept

Traditionally e-commerce sites have a strong disconnect between the identity/entertainment aspect and the functionality of a commerce experience. Through using the latest interactive technology, Glow developed a "single element" where entertainment integrates seamlessly into e-commerce.

Info

DESIGN AND PROGRAMMING: Glow Interactive <www.glowinteractive.com>. /// TOOLS: Macromedia Flash, ColdFusion, SQL server, Adobe Photoshop. /// CONTENTS: Blinde Matrix eyewear collection. /// AWARDS: FWA.

Les sites d'e-commerce ont la mauvaise habitude de dissocier l'aspect identité/divertissement de l'aspect fonctionnel d'un service d'achat. Glow a utilisé le dernier cri en matière de technologies interactives pour développer un « élément unique » où le divertissement s'intègre parfaitement à l'e-commerce. /// Traditionelle E-Commerce-Seiten trennen den unterhaltenden Aspekt von der Funktionalität eines E-Commerce-Einkaufs. Durch die Verwendung der neuesten interaktiven Technik entwickelte Glow eine Einheit, die Unterhaltung nahtlos mit E-Commerce verknüpft.

NOTNEUTRAL

www.notneutral.com

Concept

We wanted to convey the difference between the company and the product; the dual navigation and various design elements accomplish this. The other difference comes with the use of white space. Most ecommerce sites clutter the design with too much information. We wanted the products to speak for themselves; "less is more" was our design approach with notNeutral.

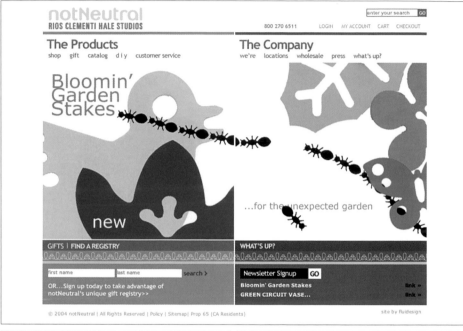

Info

DESIGN PROGRAMMING: Fluidesign <www.fluidesign.com>. /// TOOLS: CSS, PHP, Macromedia Flash, Adobe Photoshop, HTML. /// CONTENTS: photos, text, animation, e-commerce functionality. /// COST: 200 hours.

Pour exprimer la différence que nous voulions faire entre l'entreprise et le produit, nous avons utilisé une navigation en deux parties et des éléments de design distincts. L'autre différence vient de l'utilisation de l'espace blanc. La plupart des sites d'e-commerce encombrent l'espace de trop d'informations. Nous voulions que les produits parlent d'eux-mêmes. Pour notNeutral, la simplicité était au cœur de notre approche créative. /// Wir wollten den Unterschied zwischen Produkt und Unternehmen vermitteln; dies wird durch die doppelte Navigation und die vielfältigen Designelemente erreicht. Ein weiterer Unterschied entsteht durch die Verwendung weißer Flächen. Das Design der meisten E-Commerce-Seiten ist mit zu viel Informationen vollgestopft. Wir wollten, dass die Produkte für sich sprechen; unser Ansatz bei notNeutral lautete: "Weniger ist mehr".

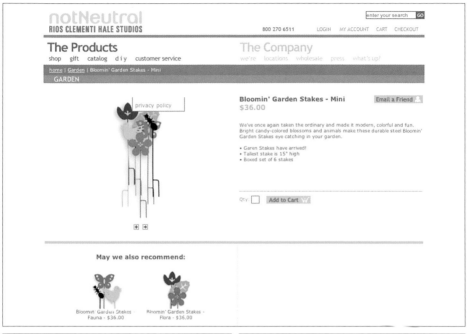

NUAN+

www.nuan.gr.jp

Concept

It is not only an online store for the selected brands of nuan+, but an visual magazine that explains the brand concept and mood of nuan+ as well.

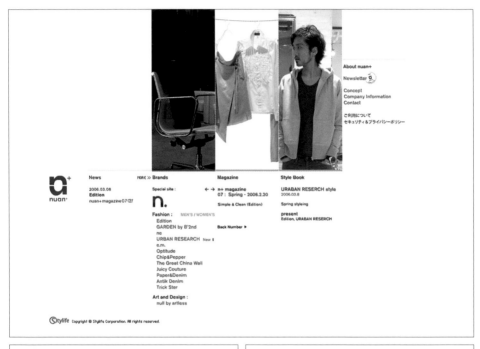

Info

DESIGN: Shun Kawakami (artless Inc.) <www.artless.gr.jp>. /// PROGRAMMING: Kiyokazu Ono. /// TOOLS: Adobe Photoshop, Adobe Illustrator, Macromedia Flash. /// CONTENTS: visual magazine and online store. /// COST: 2 months.

Ce n'est pas seulement une boutique en ligne pour les marques sélectionnées par nuan+, c'est aussi un magazine visuel qui explique le concept de la marque nuan+ et son atmosphère. /// **Dies ist nicht nur ein Online-Shop für die verschiedenen Marken von nuan+, sondern auch ein visuelles Magazin, welches das Markenkonzept von nuan+ erläutert.**

Concept

What makes this site unique is the try and buy concept. Visitors are invited to try the different typefaces in an interactive text editor. Then make their selection. The whole e-commerce aspect, ordering fonts, secure payment and downloading of the fonts acquired, happens in this same fluid Flash environment - without without having to jump out into any html payment pages - which offers a truly usable and most efficient user experience. Even the user pages, downloads and invoice history, are integrated in this one Flash application.

Info

DESIGN AND PROGRAMMING: group94 <www.group94.com>. /// TOOLS: Macromedia Freehand, Macromedia Flash, PHP, MySQL. /// CONTENTS: typefaces. /// AWARDS: FWA (site of the week), FlashKit (site of the week), WellVetted's, NewsToday (QBN), Flashforward 2004. /// COST: 2 months.

L'originalité de ce site, c'est le concept « essayez avant d'acheter ». Les visiteurs sont invités à essayer les différentes polices de caractères dans un traitement de texte interactif. Plus ils font leur choix. Tous les aspects liés à l'e-commerce, la commande des polices, le paiement sécurisé et le téléchargement des polices achetées se déroulent dans le même environnement Flash, sans devoir aller sur une page de paiement en HTML, ce qui offre un service plus efficace et facile à utiliser. Même les pages utilisateur, les téléchargements et l'historique des factures sont intégrés dans cette application Flash. /// Was diese Seite einzigartig macht, ist das "try-and-buy"-Konzept: Besucher können die verschiedenen Schriftbilder mit einem interaktiven Texteditor ausprobieren und danach ihre Wahl treffen. Der ganze Aspekt des E-Commerce – Schriftarten bestellen, sichere Bezahlung und das Herunterladen der benötigten Schriftarten – erfolgt in derselben fließenden Flash-Umgebung, ohne dass man auf andere HTML-Seiten springen muss. Dadurch ist die Seite effizient und benutzerfreundlich. Sogar die Benutzerseiten, Downloads und Rechnungsübersicht sind in diese Flash-Anwendung integriert.

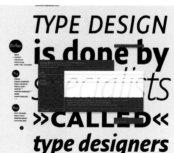

Concept

The aim of the campaign was to support PDK in entering a market of car-credits operators. Max Weber was responsible for creation of CI for PDK as well as for all possible Internet activities. Main assumption was to leave financial nomenclature in order to make communication clear and easy. We dismissed all empty and unemotional pictures and replaced them with characteristic animations. We bet on PDK's distinguishable design and innovative tools which enable users to make decision about credits.

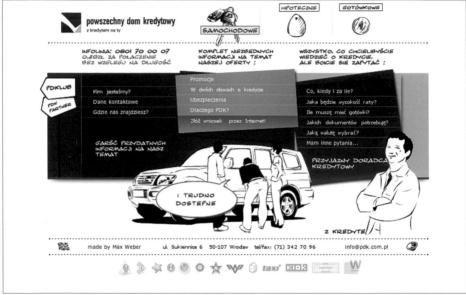

Info

DESIGN AND PROGRAMMING: Max Weber <www.maxweber.com>. /// **TOOLS:** html, Adobe Photoshop, Macromedia Flash. /// **CONTENTS:** animation. /// **AWARDS:** Cannes Cyber Lion (Gold), Golden Drum (Silver Drum), New York Festivals (Bronze World Medal), Cresta Interactive (Interactive Winner), KTR Awards, Złote Orły (Zloty Orzel), FWA (Site of the Month), Ultrashock (Bombshock). London International Awards (Shortlist), D&AD Awards, Epica Awards. /// **COST:** 1 year.

La campagne devait soutenir l'entrée de PDK sur le marché des opérateurs de crédit à l'achat de voitures. Max Weber était responsable de la création de CI pour PDK ainsi que de toutes les activités sur Internet. Il fallait surtout organiser la nomenclature financière afin de faciliter et de clarifier la communication. Nous avons écarté toutes les images vides et neutres, et nous les avons remplacées par des animations qui avaient plus de personnalité. Le site original et les outils innovants de PDK aident les utilisateurs à choisir leur crédit. /// Das Ziel dieser Kampagne bestand darin, PDK beim Eintritt in den Markt der Autokredite zu unterstützen. Max Weber war für die Entwicklung der CI für PDK sowie für alle Internetaktivitäten verantwortlich. Die finanzielle Nomenklatur wurde ausgeblendet, um die Kommunikation klar und einfach zu machen. Wir verzichteten auf alle leeren und nichtssagenden Bilder und ersetzten sie durch charakteristische Animationen. Das unverwechselbare Design und innovative Werkzeuge ermöglichen es dem Benutzer, eine Entscheidung über Kredite zu treffen.

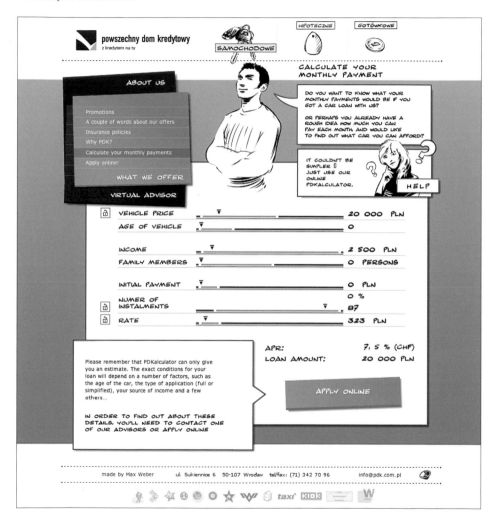

Concept

Easy to use, fast, and branded.

why look good...
when you can look per-fékt.

easy
quick
advanced technology
smooth
magnetic
multi-functional
anti-aging

skin perfection gel

The look this season is all about healthy,
glowing skin! Per-tékt's silky smooth sheer
color gel formulation 'per-tékt's' and
enhances the skin offering an alternative to
traditional foundation.

more info   purchase now

per-fékt beauty ®*

* Home
  Products
  Company
  Testimonials
  Press
  Contact

Info

DESIGN AND PROGRAMMING: Knowawall Design <www.knowawall.com>. /// TOOLS: Macromedia Flash, PHP. /// CONTENTS: photo, product info. ///
COST: 75 hours.

the company
founded 2005, Hollywood, CA

Per-fékt Beauty Inc. is fully committed to launching technologically advanced products that simplify and per-fékt beauty. Merging advanced skincare formulations with color, Per-fékt offers multi-functional products that are quick and easy to apply, long lasting, and offer an alternative to traditional foundation and beauty products. No product will be brought to market that is not within the guidelines of the company strategy. Per-fékt Beauty, Inc. promises to live up to its claims without compromise.

Read more about Richard Anderson, Founder/President Per-fékt Beauty, Inc.

Home
Products
Company
Testimonials
Press
Contact

per-fékt beauty*

Concept

The S&B Filters website offers a Flash-based filter builder enabling customers to design their own custom filter based on their car's specific requirements. The user-friendly process provides step-by-step previews of the filter throughout the design process to ensure customer satisfaction.

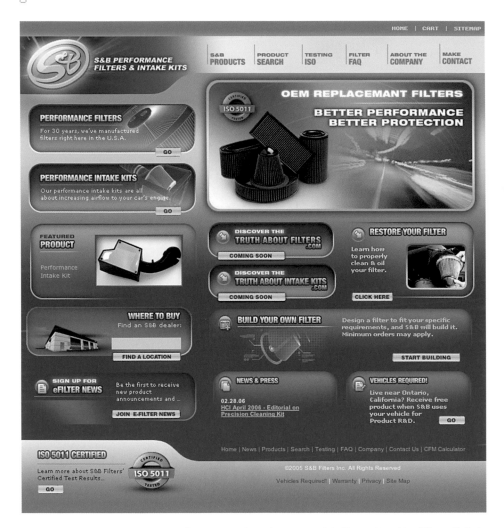

Info

DESIGN: Eric Jordan, Jonathan Moore, Elder Jerez Jr. (2Advanced Studios) <www.2advanced.com>. Project Manager: Cooper Griggs (2Advanced Studios) /// PROGRAMMING: Brad Jackson, Ryan Serra, Sonny Kotler (2Advanced Studios). /// TOOLS: Macromedia Flash, Adobe Photoshop, PHP, MySQL. /// CONTENTS: photos. /// COST: 6 months.

Le site S&B Filters propose à ses clients une application Flash qui leur permet de créer un filtre personnalisé selon les caractéristiques de leur voiture. Le processus convivial permet de visualiser le filtre à chaque étape de la création, pour la plus grande satisfaction des clients. /// Die S&B Filters-Webseite bietet einen Flash-basierten Filter-Designer, der es den Kunden ermöglicht, ihren eigenen Filter gemäß der spezifischen Erfordernisse ihrer Autos zu entwerfen. Der anwenderfreundliche Prozess bietet Schritt-für-Schritt-Vorschauen des Filters während des Designprozesses, um die Kundenzufriedenheit zu gewährleisten.

Concept Shoplifters will be prosecuted.

Info DESIGN: Carsten Schneider, Lars Eberle (Less Rain) <www.lessrain.com>. /// PROGRAMMING: Oliver Greschke (Less Rain) <www.lessrain.com>. /// TOOLS: Macromedia Freehand, Macromedia Flash MX, php, Html, PayPal. /// CONTENTS: illustration, animation, photography, sound, and music. /// COST: 230 hours.

SHOP COMPOSITION

USA

www.shopcomposition.com

2005

Concept High-quality, large-format product images are a dominant element throughout the site; filling the screen, providing both texture and visual interest. While most checkouts bounce visitors between pages, the flash checkout process creates a seamless three-step process. Visitors can easily view and modify cart and checkout information without ever having to repost data or use the back button; it's not only faster, it's less confusing.

SHOP BY VENDOR | kisim

There are women who choose their handbags, There are handbags who choose their women. Kisim's strong, independent designs are enjoyed by strong, independent women around the world. The line is based in Isreal and features designs that beautifully combine classic materials and progressive styling.

VIEW FULL PRODUCT LINE
CLICK HERE TO VIEW >>

composition

C

search   store   policies

shop composition

kisim   for work

shopping cart   0 items

Newsletter Signup
New additions coming soon - sign up for our

Info DESIGN AND PROGRAMMING: Ian Coyle. /// TOOLS: Macromedia Flash (XML), Adobe Photoshop, ASP.net (xml), Custom CMS (orderprocessing tool). /// CONTENTS: modern goods and products e-commerce site. /// AWARDS: Communication Arts Interactive, Clios Shortlist 2005, FWA (Site of The Day Award 2005), Flash Forward 2005 (Finalist), SXSW 2005 (Finalist), Forbes Best of Web (Winner), Flash in the Can 2005 (Finalist), TINY (Site of the month). /// COST: 125 hours.

Le principal élément du site, ce sont les images des produits. Grand format et haute définition, elles remplissent l'écran et donnent à la fois de la texture et un intérêt visuel. Alors que la plupart des sites renvoient les visiteurs de page en page lors de la partie achat, ici le processus se déroule en trois étapes intégrées grâce à Flash. Les visiteurs peuvent facilement voir et modifier leur panier et leurs données personnelles sans devoir revalider ni revenir en arrière. Ce n'est pas seulement plus rapide, c'est aussi beaucoup plus agréable. /// Hochwertige, großformatige Bilder der Produkte dominieren die gesamte Seite; sie füllen den Bildschirm aus, geben der Seite eine Gestalt und erzeugen visuelles Interesse. Während Besucher beim Checkout meist zwischen verschiedenen Seiten wechseln müssen, ermöglicht Flash einen nahtlosen Prozess in drei Schritten. Besucher können Einkaufswagen und Informationen leicht einsehen und verändern, ohne wiederholt Daten eingeben oder den Rückwärts-Knopf anklicken zu müssen – das ist nicht nur einfacher, sondern auch weniger verwirrend.

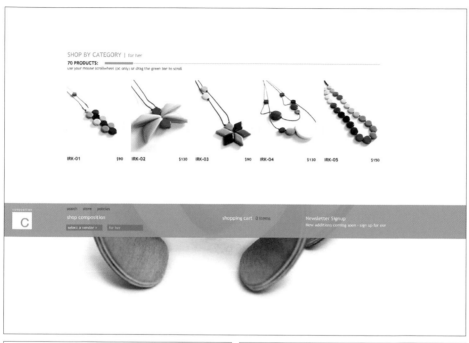

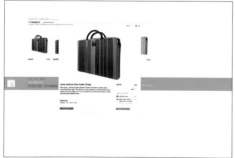
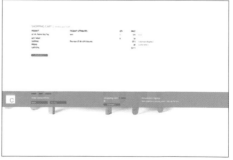

Concept

Shufflesome's offering achieves the best possible fit with user's demands by providing the incentives and tools to develop the product (sticker artwork for the iPod) on your own. The offering is by users for users. The website's experience is composed to give individual creators the ability to use Shufflesome for self-promotion that finds worldwide reponse.

Info

DESIGN AND PROGRAMMING: Alexander Schneider <http://reflect.typepad.com/jg>. /// TOOLS: Typepad (www.typepad.com), Adobe Photoshop, TextEdit, CSS, HTML. /// CONTENTS: graphics and photos.

L'offre de Shufflesome s'ajuste au mieux aux préférences de l'utilisateur en l'incitant à développer le produit (des autocollants pour habiller l'iPod) lui-même et en lui fournissant les outils pour le faire. Par les utilisateurs, pour les utilisateurs. Le site permet aux différents créateurs d'utiliser Shufflesome pour se faire de la publicité dans le monde entier. /// Shufflesome entspricht den Ansprüchen der Benutzer auf die bestmögliche Weise: Es bietet Ideen und Werkzeuge, um das Produkt (Stickervorlagen für iPods) eigenständig zu entwickeln. Das Angebot ist von Benutzern für Benutzer. Die Webseite verschafft einzelnen Designern die Möglichkeit, sich mithilfe von Shufflesome zu präsentieren, und erhält weltweite Resonanz.

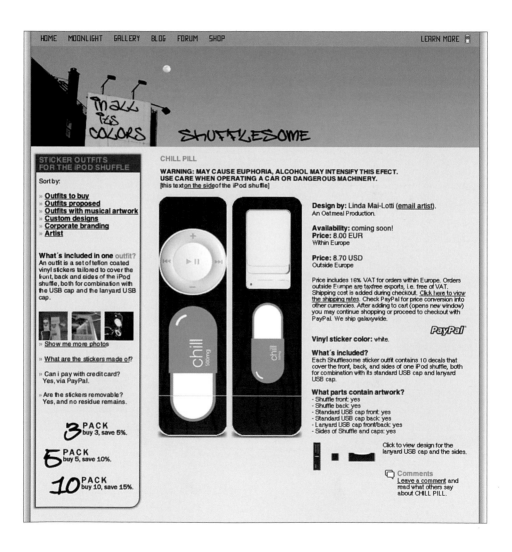

Concept

A beautiful and user-friendly shopping experience for something as simple as caravans. Siblu is the new name for Haven Europe and has leapfrogged their competition and established itself as a holiday leader. The site uses intelligent content to customise user experiences and is completed maintained by Siblu thanks to the Large CMS.

Info

DESIGN: Large <www.largedesign.com>. /// PROGRAMMING: Front-end and Content Management System by Large. Booking engine by Xko <www.xko.co.uk>. /// TOOLS: Adobe Photoshop, Macromedia Flash, Adobe Illustrator, PHP, MySql. /// COST: 1.500 hours.

Ou comment faire de l'achat d'un produit aussi simple qu'une caravane une expérience belle et conviviale. Siblu est le nouveau nom de Haven Europe et a dépassé la concurrence en s'établissant comme leader dans le secteur des vacances. Ce site utilise un contenu intelligent pour personnaliser les visites des utilisateurs, et le puissant système de gestion des contenus permet à Siblu de l'administrer entièrement. /// Ein schönes und benutzerfreundliches Einkaufserlebnis, so simpel wie Wohnwagen. Siblu ist der neue Namen für Haven Europe, der seine Konkurrenz überholt und sich als führender Urlaubsanbieter etabliert hat. Der Inhalt der Seite ist intelligent und auf individuelle Benutzererlebnisse zugeschnitten. Die Seite wird dank des CMS von Large komplett von Siblu gewartet.

Concept

The site allows the user to fully customize a SoccerTed key ring. Using a flash interface the user can drag and drop colours, choose kit designs, heads, and attachments. The unique design choices are then stored and passed to a shopping basket. When the order is received an identifier code is pasted into a flash application to visualize the design.

S⚽ccerTed

SoccerTed is a beautifully hand-crafted,
personalised, solid silver collectible.

This website requires the latest Flash player. Download it here.

Enter to design your own SoccerTed.

Info

DESIGN: Matt Rice, Hege Aaby (Sennep) <www.sennep.com>. /// PROGRAMMING: Thomas Poeser, Mikkel Askjaer. /// TOOLS: Macromedia Flash, Macromedia Freehand, Adobe Photoshop, PHP, MySQL, PayPal. /// CONTENTS: photographic showcase, product information, customizable key ring application. /// COST: 1 month.

Le site permet de personnaliser un porte-clés SoccerTed. Dans l'interface Flash, on peut glisser-déplacer les couleurs, choisir différents motifs, différentes têtes et différents accessoires. La création originale est ensuite enregistrée dans le panier d'achats. Lorsque la commande est reçue, un code d'identification est copié dans une application Flash pour visualiser le produit créé. /// Diese Seite ermöglicht es dem Anwender, einen SoccerTed-Schlüsselring nach eigenen Wünschen zu gestalten. Mithilfe einer Flash-Oberfläche kann der Benutzer mit Drag & Drop Farben, Designs und Zubehör auswählen. Die individuelle Design-Auswahl wird gespeichert und in einen Einkaufskorb gelegt. Nach der Bestellung wird ein Identifizierungscode in eine Flash-Applikation gespeist und so das Design sichtbar.

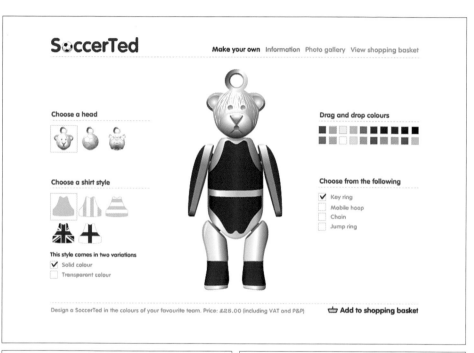

SUNGLASS HUT

www.sunglasshut.com

Concept

Sunglass Hut has over 2,000 stores in the US. Their success has been down to convenience and choice in their shops. Their involvement with Miami Swimshows and Large's work has made them a fashion destination site with lots of great fashion stories, pictures and products. Check out 'Are you famous' launching soon...

Info

DESIGN: Large <www.largedesign.com>. /// **PROGRAMMING:** Front-end and Content Management System by Large. /// **TOOLS:** Adobe Photoshop, Macromedia Flash, Adobe Illustrator, PHP, MySql. /// **COST:** 900 hours.

Sunglass Hut a plus de 2 000 boutiques aux États-Unis. Leur succès est dû à la commodité de leurs boutiques et au grand choix qu'elles proposent. Leur parte-nariat avec Miami Swimshows et le travail de Large a fait de leur site une destination à la mode, avec des tas d'histoires, de photos et de produits. Allez voir la partie « Are you famous » (êtes-vous célèbre), bientôt disponible... /// **Sunglass Hut** besitzt über 2 000 Läden in den USA. Ihr Erfolg basiert auf Komfort und großer Auswahl. Ihre Einbindung von Miami Swimshows und Larges Arbeiten hat sie zu einer Modeseite gemacht, die viele Modegeschichten, Bilder und Produkte zeigt. Halten Sie die Augen offen nach "Are you famous"...

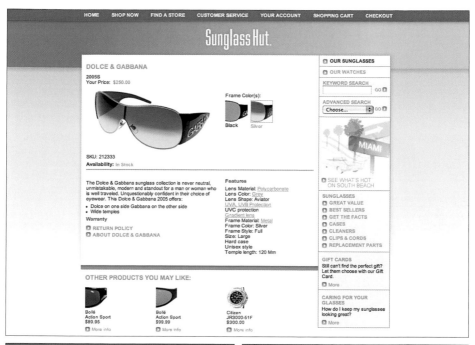

SURF RIDE

www.surfride.com

Concept The Surf Ride website boasts two Flash-based modules enabling customers to customize skateboards and wakeboards prior to purchase. The skateboard builder allows customers to select from various hardware options, such as wheels and bearings, to create the ultimate ride. The wakeboard builder also gives customers various board and bindings options. Both offer a quick, step-by-step process with a preview of the customized product to ensure customer satisfaction.

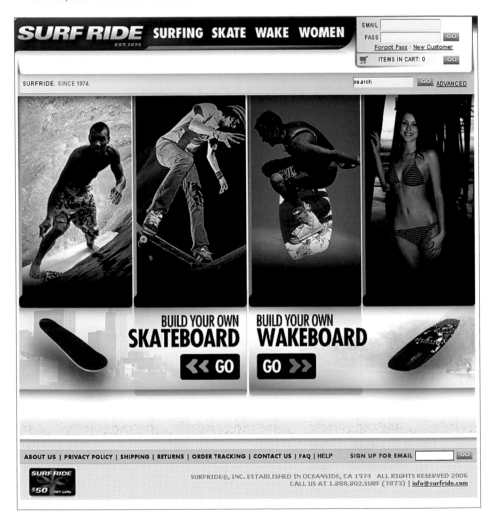

Info DESIGN: Brad Jackson (2Advanced Studios) <www.2advanced.com>, Project Manager: Cooper Griggs (2Advanced Studios). /// PROGRAMMING: Brad Jackson, Ryan Serra (2Advanced Studios). /// TOOLS: Macromedia Flash, PHP, Adobe Photoshop. /// CONTENTS: photos. /// COST: 3 months.

Le site de Surf Ride possède deux modules en Flash qui proposent aux clients de personnaliser leurs planches de skateboard et leur wakeboard avant de les acheter. Le module des planches de skateboard offre aux clients un grand choix d'options, comme les roues et les roulements. Le module des wakeboards offre aussi différentes options de planches et de fixations. Le processus est rapide, étape par étape, et propose une prévisualisation du produit personnalisé afin de garantir la satisfaction du client. /// Die Surf Ride-Webseite rühmt sich zweier Flash-basierter Module, die es dem Kunden ermöglichen, Skateboards und Wakeboards vor dem Kauf seinen eigenen Wünschen anzupassen. Beim Bau eines Skateboards kann der Kunde zwischen verschiedenen Hardware-Optionen, wie Reifen und Lager, wählen. Der Bau der Wakeboards basiert auf einem schnellen Schritt-für-Schritt-Prozess mit einer Vorschau des individuell gestalteten Produkts zur Gewährleistung der Kundenzufriedenheit.

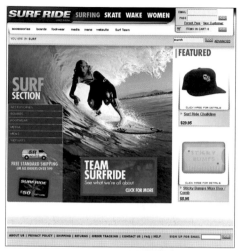

THEORY7 FLASH STORE

www.theory7.com

Concept
Site features the worlds first fully featured 100% flash forum as well as the first real-time credit card processing system with fully integrated flash shopping cart and automated product delivery system.

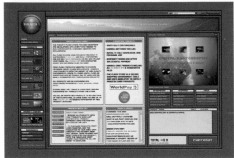

Info
DESIGN: Nevil Slade [Theory7 Ltd]. /// **PROGRAMMING:** John Harry. /// **TOOLS:** Macromedia Flash MX, Flash Comm Server, PHP and MYSQL, ASP and MSSQL. /// **CONTENTS:** photos, flash games, music loops, flash forums, pre built flash interfaces, flash applications, guestbook, portfolio. /// **AWARDS:** FWA [Site of the Month and Site of the Year], Flash Move, FlashKit [Site of the Day], TINY [Site of the Week], Fcukstar, DOPE Awards, NewWebPick. /// **COST:** 4.000 hours.

Ce site présente le premier forum entièrement en Flash ainsi que le premier système de traitement de cartes de crédit en temps réel avec un panier d'achats intégré en Flash et un système de livraison automatisé. /// Diese Seite beinhaltet das weltweit erste voll ausgestattete 100%-ige Flash-Forum sowie das erste Echtzeit-Kreditkartensystem mit integriertem Flash-Einkaufswagen und automatisiertem Produktlieferungssystem.

THREADLESS

www.threadless.com

Concept

Threadless is a community-based online tee shirt business. A community of over 250,000 users submit tee shirt designs, which are scored for 7 days. The top scoring designs (4-6 per week) are printed and sold on the site. The winning designer gets $1,000 (US). All aspects of the site are controlled and contributed by the community.

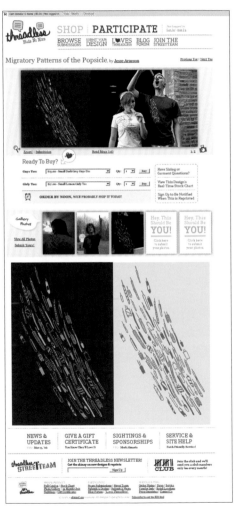

Info

DESIGN: Jeffrey Kalmikoff (skinnyCorp) <www.skinnycorp.com>. /// PROGRAMMING: Jake Nickell, Jacob DeHart (skinnyCorp). /// TOOLS: PHP, MySql, Custom CMS, Adobe Photoshop, Adobe Illustrator, Macromedia Flash. /// CONTENTS: photos, tee-shirt design submissions. /// AWARDS: Cool Homepages, Macromedia Site of the Day.

Threadless se base sur le principe de la communauté pour vendre ses T-shirts. Une communauté de plus de 250 000 utilisateurs soumet des idées de T-shirts, qui sont ensuite soumises à notation pendant sept jours. Les créations les mieux notées (de quatre à six par semaine) sont imprimées et vendues sur le site. Leur créateur gagne 1 000 USD. La communauté ne fait pas que participer à tous les aspects du site, elle en a aussi le contrôle. /// Threadless basiert auf einer Community, die online T-Shirts vertreibt. Eine Gemeinde von über 250 000 Benutzern stellt T-Shirt-Designs vor, die 7 Tage lang bewertet werden. Die am besten bewerteten (4-6 pro Woche) werden auf der Seite gedruckt und verkauft. Der Gewinner erhält $1 000. Die Benutzergemeinde liefert alle Beiträge zur Seite und kontrolliert alle Aspekte.

☐ Cart Details: 1 Items | $15.00 | Not logged in | View / Modify | Checkout

SHOP | PARTICIPATE

Not Logged In
Log In | Join Us

| SHOP OUR FULL | WHAT'S IN | PHOTO | 12 MONTH | DESIGNER |
| CATALOG | STOCK? | GALLERY | CLUB | INTERVIEWS |

How much do you love your friends?

Select the amount you wish to give to add a gift certificate to your shopping cart. Though no paper gift certificate will be physically sent, after you check out you will have the ability to either print the gift certificate for giving or to send it via e-mail as an e-card!

Not Too Much
You're either a cheap-o or have very little money and want to show your friends a little love.

Give a $25 Gift Certificate |

More Than Most
50 bucks is pretty good! Not the most to give, but definitely more than enough!

Give a $50 Gift Certificate |

A Whole Helluva Lot
You are the best friend ever! Luckily there's no such thing as too many tee shirts.

Give a $100 Gift Certificate |

| NEWS & UPDATES | GIVE A GIFT CERTIFICATE | SIGHTINGS & SPONSORSHIPS | SERVICE & SITE HELP |
| UPD: Mar 13, '06 | You Know They'll Love It | UPD: Mark Almaria | Fast & Friendly Service! |

JOIN THE THREADLESS NEWSLETTER!
Get the skinny on new designs & reprints

Sign Up |

Join the club and we'll send you a club members only tee every month!

SHOP & PRODUCT
Full Catalog | Stock Chart
Photo Gallery | 12 Month Club
Sightings | Gift Certificates

PARTICIPATE
Score Submissions | Street Team
Submit A Design | Submit A Photo
Blog Forum | "Loves Threadless"

SERVICE & INFO
Order Status | News | Service
Vendor Info | Retail Locations
Press Inquiries | Contact Us

© 2006, a skinnyCorp company. All designs Copyright by owner. Subscribe to our tee RSS feed!

Concept

We like to boost creativity and show the great products in this world. Our drive is authenticity, fairness, innovativity, difference, clarity and resistance. In this way we like to support artists and establish an alternative to the mass consumption.

Info

DESIGN: VFX Johow (Handmade) <http://vfxjohow.johow.com>; <http://handmade.johow.com>. /// PROGRAMMING: Handmade. /// TOOLS: PHP, HTML. /// CONTENTS: photos, slide show. /// COST: 200 hours.

Nous aimons stimuler la créativité et présenter les meilleurs produits. Nos mots d'ordre sont authenticité, équité, innovation, différence, clarté et résistance. C'est ainsi que nous souhaitons soutenir les artistes et donner une alternative à la consommation de masse. /// Wir erhöhen Kreativität und präsentieren die besten Produkte der Welt. Wir streben nach Authentizität, Fairness, Innovation, Einzigartigkeit, Klarheit und Beständigkeit. Auf diese Art unterstützen wir Künstler und bieten eine Alternative zum Massenkonsum.

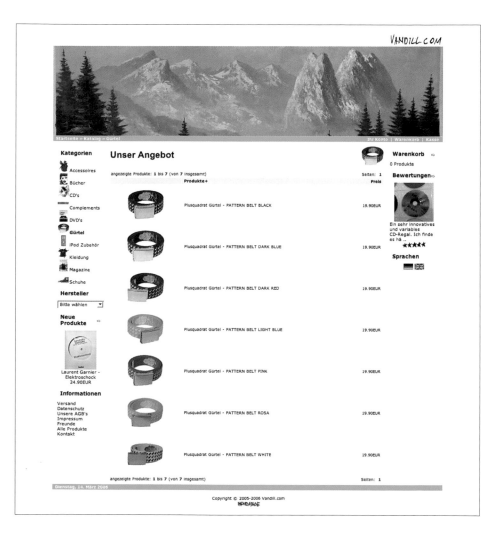

THE WIRED STORE

www.wiredstore.net

2005

With Tivo changing the face of traditional advertising, brands need to find new ways to extend advertising for their brands... enter immersive advertising. This e-commerce site blurs the boundaries between content and commercials. The entire experience is clean, smooth and fun to explore, yet it is essentially an interactive advertisment.

DESIGN: Diet Strychnine Corp <www.dietstrychnine.com>. /// **PROGRAMMING:** Chris Daou (Diet Strychnine Corp). /// **TOOLS:** Adobe Photoshop, Adobe Illustrator, Macromedia Flash, Mochibot. /// **CONTENTS:** photos. /// **COST:** 300 hours.

Depuis Tivo, la publicité traditionnelle n'est plus la même : les marques doivent trouver une nouvelle visibilité... Elles doivent entrer dans la publicité d'immersion. Ce site d'e-commerce efface les limites entre le contenu et les publicités. Il est clair, facile à utiliser et drôle à explorer, et pourtant c'est surtout une publicité interactive. /// Seit Tivo das Gesicht der traditionellen Werbung änderte, suchen Marken nach neuen Möglichkeiten für die eigene Werbung... ihr Einstieg in effektive Werbemaßnahmen. Diese E-Commerce-Seite lässt die Grenzen zwischen Inhalt und Werbung verschwimmen. Das gesamte Erlebnis ist technisch einwandfrei, und es macht Spaß, die Seite zu entdecken, obwohl sie im Wesentlichen aus interaktiver Werbung besteht.

WOMENSECRET.COM

www.womensecret.com

Concept

womensecret.com is much more than just an e-commerce web site. It's a space created specially for women. Women who are dynamic, involved and committed. Women with an interest in culture, fashion and the latest trends. Women who love discovering and trying out new things and above all experiencing new sensations. Womensecret.com is divided into two clearly differentiated sections: the on-line store and the contents section, where a simple search will reveal our truly magical side.

Info

DESIGN: Andreu Colomer and Sergi Mula (minnim). /// PROGRAMMING: Javier Álvarez and Carles Sanz (minnim). /// TOOLS: Macromedia Flash, XML, ASP, Adobe Photoshop, Macromedia Freehand. /// CONTENTS: photo, music, film.

Womensecret.com est bien plus qu'un simple site d'e-commerce. C'est un espace créé tout spécialement pour les femmes. Des femmes dynamiques, engagées et responsables. Des femmes qui s'intéressent à la culture, à la mode et aux dernières tendances. Des femmes qui aiment découvrir et tester les nouveautés et surtout les nouvelles sensations. Womensecret.com est composé de deux sections bien distinctes : la boutique en ligne et la section des contenus, où une simple recherche révélera notre véritable magie. /// womensecret.com ist viel mehr als eine bloße E-Commerce-Webseite. Sie ist ein Ort speziell für Frauen – Frauen, die dynamisch und engagiert sind. Frauen mit Interesse an Kultur, Mode und den neuesten Trends. Frauen, die Neues entdecken möchten und ausprobieren und gerne neue Erfahrungen machen. Womensecret.com ist in zwei klar zu unterscheidende Bereiche geteilt: den Online-Shop und den Inhaltsbereich, wo eine einfache Suche unsere wahrhaft magische Seite enthüllt.

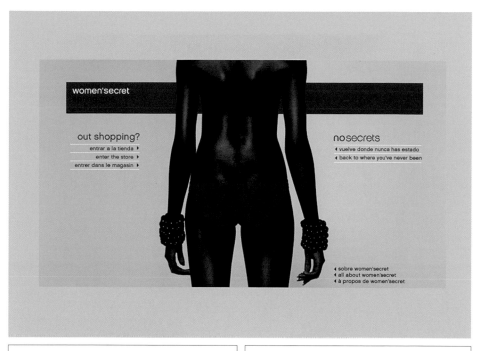

I would like to thank all studios and professionals participating in the book again, as well all people
involved, for their contribution and effort to provide the
materials and information that enriched this publication. Also Daniel Siciliano Brêtas for his work designing
and layouting the book. His work has been fundamental
to make this a great inspirational book. Moreover, Stefan
Klatte for guiding us always in the technical details and
helping us making a better job every day. This volume
has taken a step further from the other three volumes.
As the subject e-commerce involves a lot of technical,
marketing and design aspects that should work all
together, we invited 7 top design offices and companies
to present their experience building up an online branch
of specific businesses.

For that, I want to send my special thanks to Tony
Novak from 2Advanced, Luba Shekhter from Firstborn,
David Lai from Hello Design, David Skokna from Huge,
Lars Hemming Jorgensen from Large Design, Ralf
Burghart from Machinas, and Alex Koch from WYSIWYG.
These professionals know what they do and what they
talk about. Their successful experiences will certainly
encourage you to think about your future initiatives.

It was also a pleasure to be able to feature a
site that I am a regular customer. Germanwings
<www.germanwings.com> is not only a brilliant corpora-
tion, it has a magnificent site that I use regularly to fly
from Cologne to nearly any point in Europe. I buy just
online and until today I have never had a single problem.

The amazing thing these days is that we are located in
different cities and continents, and the only person I met
in Person was Alex, that is based in Düsseldorf. We never
had a problem to work together. A brief introduction via
e-mail enables us to built solid relationships and share
ideas, dreams and gets the work done.

Learning from success is the message of the book!

Julius Wiedemann

Web Design: E-commerce

To stay informed about upcoming TASCHEN titles, please request our magazine at www.taschen.com/magazine or write to TASCHEN, Hohenzollernring 53, D-50672 Cologne, Germany, contact@taschen.com, Fax: +49-221-254919. We will be happy to send you a free copy of our magazine which is filled with information about all of our books.

Design & Layout: Daniel Siciliano Brêtas
Production: Stefan Klatte

Editor: Julius Wiedemann
Assitant-editor: Daniel Siciliano Brêtas
French Translation: Aurélie Daniel
German Translation: Claudia Dziallas
Spanish Translation: María del Mar Portillo
Italian Translation: Marco Barberi
Portuguese Translation: Alcides Murtinheira

Printed in Italy
ISBN 978-3-8228-4055-9

TASCHEN is not responsible when web addresses cannot be reached if they are offline or can be viewed just with plug-ins.

Web Design: Music Sites
Ed. Julius Wiedemann / Flexi-
cover, 192 pp. / € 6.99 /
$ 9.99 / £ 5.99 / ¥ 1.500

Web Design: Flash Sites
Ed. Julius Wiedemann / Flexi-
cover, 192 pp. / € 6.99 /
$ 9.99 / £ 5.99 / ¥ 1.500

Web Design: Portfolios
Ed. Julius Wiedemann / Flexi-
cover, 192 pp. / € 6.99 /
$ 9.99 / £ 5.99 / ¥ 1.500

"These books are beautiful objects, well-designed and lucid." —*Le Monde*, Paris, on the ICONS series

" Buy them all and add some pleasure to your life."

60s Fashion
Ed. Jim Heimann

70s Fashion
Ed. Jim Heimann

African Style
Ed. Angelika Taschen

Alchemy & Mysticism
Alexander Roob

American Indian
Dr. Sonja Schierle

Angels
Gilles Néret

Architecture Now!
Ed. Philip Jodidio

Art Now
Eds. Burkhard Riemschneider,
Uta Grosenick

Atget's Paris
Ed. Hans Christian Adam

Bamboo Style
Ed. Angelika Taschen

Ingrid Bergman
Ed. Paul Duncan, Scott Eyman

Berlin Style
Ed. Angelika Taschen

Humphrey Bogart
Ed. Paul Duncan, James Ursini

Marlon Brando
Ed. Paul Duncan,
F.X. Feeney

Brussels Style
Ed. Angelika Taschen

Cars of the 50s
Ed. Jim Heimann,
Tony Thacker

Cars of the 60s
Ed. Jim Heimann, Tony Thacker

Cars of the 70s
Ed. Jim Heimann, Tony Thacker

Charlie Chaplin
Ed. Paul Duncan, David Robinson

China Style
Ed. Angelika Taschen

Christmas
Ed. Jim Heimann, Steven Heller

Design Handbook
Charlotte & Peter Fiell

Design for the 21ˢᵗ Century
Eds. Charlotte & Peter Fiell

Design of the 20ᵗʰ Century
Eds. Charlotte & Peter Fiell

Marlene Dietrich
Ed. Paul Duncan,
James Ursini

Devils
Gilles Néret

Robert Doisneau
Ed. Jean-Claude Gautrand

East German Design
Ralf Ulrich/Photos: Ernst Hedler

Clint Eastwood
Ed. Paul Duncan, Douglas
Keesey

Egypt Style
Ed. Angelika Taschen

Encyclopaedia Anatomica
Ed. Museo La Specola Florence

M.C. Escher

Fashion
Ed. The Kyoto Costume Institute

Fashion Now!
Eds. Terry Jones, Susie Rushton

Fruit
Ed. George Brookshaw,
Uta Pellgrü-Gagel

HR Giger
HR Giger

Grand Tour
Harry Seidler

Cary Grant
Ed. Paul Duncan, F.X. Feeney

Graphic Design
Eds. Charlotte & Peter Fiell

Greece Style
Ed. Angelika Taschen

Halloween
Ed. Jim Heimann,
Steven Heller

Havana Style
Ed. Angelika Taschen

Audrey Hepburn
Ed. Paul Duncan, F.X. Feeney

Katharine Hepburn
Ed. Paul Duncan, Alain Silver

Homo Art
Gilles Néret

Hot Rods
Ed. Coco Shinomiya, Tony
Thacker

Hula
Ed. Jim Heimann

India Bazaar
Samantha Harrison, Bari Kumar

London Style
Ed. Angelika Taschen

Steve McQueen
Ed. Paul Duncan, Alain Silver

Mexico Style
Ed. Angelika Taschen

Miami Style
Ed. Angelika Taschen

Minimal Style
Ed. Angelika Taschen

Marilyn Monroe
Ed. Paul Duncan,
F.X. Feeney

Morocco Style
Ed. Angelika Taschen

New York Style
Ed. Angelika Taschen

Paris Style
Ed. Angelika Taschen

Penguin
Frans Lanting

20ᵗʰ Century Photography
Museum Ludwig Cologne

Pierre et Gilles
Eric Troncy

Provence Style
Ed. Angelika Taschen

Robots & Spaceships
Ed. Teruhisa Kitahara

Safari Style
Ed. Angelika Taschen

Seaside Style
Ed. Angelika Taschen

Signs
Ed. Julius Wiedeman

South African Style
Ed. Angelika Taschen

Starck
Philippe Starck

Surfing
Ed. Jim Heimann

Sweden Style
Ed. Angelika Taschen

Tattoos
Ed. Henk Schiffmacher

Tiffany
Jacob Baal-Teshuva

Tokyo Style
Ed. Angelika Taschen

Tuscany Style
Ed. Angelika Taschen

Valentines
Ed. Jim Heimann,
Steven Heller

Web Design: Best Studios
Ed. Julius Wiedemann

Web Design: Best Studios 2
Ed. Julius Wiedemann

Web Design: E-Commerce
Ed. Julius Wiedemann

Web Design: Flash Sites
Ed. Julius Wiedemann

Web Design: Music Sites
Ed. Julius Wiedemann

Web Design: Portfolios
Ed. Julius Wiedemann

Orson Welles
Ed. Paul Duncan,
F.X. Feeney

Women Artists
in the 20th and 21st Century
Ed. Uta Grosenick